WRITING
SCIENCE
FICTION

WRITING SCIENCE FICTION

Christopher Evans

St. Martin's Press
New York

Library of Congress Cataloging-in-Publication Data

Evans, Christopher.
    Writing science fiction / by Christopher Evans.
        p.   cm.
    ISBN 0-312-01849-5 : $10.95
    1. Science fiction—Authorship.   I. Title.
PN3377.5.S3E9 1988
808.3′876—dc19   87-36688
                                                              CIP

First published in Great Britain by A&C Black Ltd.

First U.S. Edition

10 9 8 7 6 5 4 3 2 1

Contents

WRITING
SCIENCE
FICTION

Introduction

If you have opened this book, you have declared an interest in the writing of science fiction. You may be wondering how to begin, or you may have actually started writing stories but are having difficulties with them. Or you may simply be looking for a short-cut to instant bestsellerdom.

Guide books on writing can be very alluring to new writers, holding out the promise that they contain all the secrets of success. You merely have to absorb their wisdom and you will immediately progress to levels of technical and artistic expertise such that publishers will be falling over themselves to acquire your work.

Not true, of course.

It has to be said at the outset that no book can teach you how to write. The most important step to take is to begin writing, and the best way of developing your craft is to do as much of it as possible. Practise as much as you can. You will encounter plenty of problems, but finding ways of solving them yourself will teach you far more than any amount of studying 'how to' texts before you have written a single word.

On a very basic level, writing is much like driving: no one would expect to get into a car and drive off without first learning how to steer, change gear, read road signs, and so on. The same applies to writing of any sort. You need to become accustomed to using language within the context and conventions of your chosen field of writing. The difference is that you can practise on your own and develop at a pace which suits you. The corresponding danger is that, without any help at all, you may suffer constant frustrations which lead to complete disillusionment.

This is where guide books on writing can be useful. By identifying typical problems and suggesting strategies for overcoming them, they can reduce much of the heartbreak and sheer hard work involved in acquiring a good grasp of the basics of the craft. They can never have all the answers, because writing isn't an exact science and because every writer is different. However, the techniques of fiction have evolved over the centuries into a loose set of broadly accepted principles for portraying an imagined reality through prose. There is a pool of common wisdom from which all writers can draw to their benefit. This book is about the writing of science fiction, a particular kind of fiction for which certain skills and interests are needed, and in which particular problems arise. However, it is important to remember that it is a species of fiction like any other, and that the basic requirements of literacy, imagination and narrative skill are always desirable. Too much is often made of the notion that science fiction is different in the sense that it is not subject to ordinary literary criteria. Science fiction *is* different, but it is a difference in emphasis rather than fundamentals: you have to be able to write well to produce good science fiction. For this reason, many of the topics covered in this book aren't specific to the field but apply generally.

What is science fiction?

The easiest answer to this question is that it is a publisher's label to help readers identify what they want. Definitions of sf (the preferred form of abbreviaton in the field is sf rather than sci-fi, which smacks of trendiness or seems dismissive) are many and varied. It has been called everything from 'a literature of cognitive estrangement' to 'bug-eyed monster fiction', and no one has yet succeeded in coming up with a definition which pleases everyone. Largely this is due to the very protean nature of the genre: it embraces everything from crude interplanetary romances to sophisticated social and psychological dramas which may be scarcely distinguishable from uncategorised fiction. These days it is more diverse than ever.

Nevertheless, there are certain books to which we can point and categorically say 'that's science fiction'. Perhaps the crispest definition is that science fiction is a literature of 'what if?' What if we could travel in time? What if we were living on other planets? What if we made contact with alien races? And so on. The starting point is that the writer supposes things are different from how we know them to be.

Science fiction, then, is a literature of supposition. It makes one, or many, speculative leaps, *but it always endeavours to provide a logical rationale for its speculations.* This is where it differs from its close cousin, fantasy. A story set in a world where magic exists would normally qualify as fantasy; but if the writer developed a quasi-scientific theory to explain how magic works – for example, that it is a paranormal ability of the human brain – then the story might be seen as science fiction because it introduces constraints on the idea of magic so that it can't be used arbitrarily. This idea of *internal consistency* is another hallmark of sf, and the wilder the speculation, the more incumbent it is on the author to provide a set of parameters which readers can use as reference points. In this respect, science fiction is aptly named since it acknowledges – in principle, at least – the notion of a logical system underpinning its sometimes outrageous flights of fancy.

Another way of looking at science fiction is to see it as a literature of perspectives. By presenting realities which are different from those we know – the imagined future, the altered present, the past in which history was different – it can often highlight trends and assumptions in the real world, to stimulating effect. Its writers are perennially interested in *possibilities* and *potentials*. Sometimes they seek to warn us against dangerous present-day tendencies in cautionary tales which carry the implicit message 'If this goes on, then terrible things might happen'. Other writers are simply fascinated by the prospects for the human race as technology grows more and more sophisticated and more and more of the universe is explored. Others just want to tell a rattling good yarn and are attracted to sf because of its sheer inventiveness and scope for exotic settings and incidents.

What all these writers have in common is that they find ordinary reality a little too dull for their tastes. The best science fiction offers an escape from the mundane, the everyday; it provides the reader with a 'sense of wonder' – an exciting feeling of confronting new ideas and situations, or old ideas and situations presented in new ways. It subverts the status quo.

The emphasis in this book is on the practicalities of writing science fiction from both creative and commercial standpoints. Chapter 1 outlines the wide range of subjects covered by sf and how they have typically been dealt with by writers. Chapter 2 examines ideas as the raw material for stories and discusses how they can be cultivated. Chapter 3 explores plots and various aspects of narration such as viewpoint, texture and style. Chapter 4 considers characters, without whom there would be no story. Chapter 5 contains an early draft of a short story, prefaced by a description of how the idea for it arose, and followed by a brief analysis of its main flaws. Chapter 6 deals with rewriting, an essential part of the writer's craft, which is looked at both in general terms and with reference to the sample story. Finally, Chapter 7 considers what happens after a story is written and submitted for publication.

What do you need to begin?

It has already been stressed that if you want to be a writer, then you must start to write. For this, no more than pen and paper is needed at the outset, though a typewriter will probably be necessary at some point if you intend to make a career of writing. But these are just technical aids. What is far more important is the attitude and application which you bring to your writing. A measure of talent is obviously desirable, but it is absolutely vital to have the right kind of temperament. You need to be dedicated and determined. Success in writing, as has often been pointed out, is more a matter of perspiration than inspiration. The more innate ability you have, the quicker you are likely to get published and the more rewarding the work you are likely to produce. But no amount of talent can substitute for the hard graft that is also necessary to become a writer. It is a process that usually involves repeated frustrations and disappointments. You will need to be strong-willed and maintain a firm belief that in the end you will succeed.

Most writers hope for both financial and critical success, but it is important to be realistic about these possibilities. In fact, very few writers become rich; that the few are often interviewed on television and in magazines tends to give a distorted impression of their number. For every bestselling author, there are hundreds of others who barely scrape a living or have to have other jobs to support themselves. Critical respectability is also elusive, especially if you write in a field such as science fiction, which is not considered a serious form of literature by many. The best reason for wanting to become a writer is that you have a passion or even obsession for writing. This will help you overcome the disappointments you are almost certain to encounter; you will keep going because you can't help it.

Given sufficient talent (it need not be a lot) and determination (you will need plenty of it) there is a good chance that you will succeed finally in getting your work published. Being published is the criterion most often used by other people to judge whether you are any good as a writer, though this is in fact a very questionable basis for such a judgement. If you want to write purely for your own satisfaction without taking any commercial considerations into account, then fine. But most writers do write with publication in mind because they wish to communicate with as many people as possible. And for the purposes of this book the assumption is made that publication is your ultimate aim. But even publication itself won't mean that you have learned all there is to know about writing; that sort of attitude breeds complacency and stagnation. Writers never stop learning; their apprenticeship lasts as long as they continue to write.

1
The Scope of Science Fiction

Science fiction is a literature concerned with change, and the genre has its antecedents in books written as the Industrial Revolution began to affect people's lives in widespread and dramatic ways. New technological developments led to upheavals in all spheres of life, and it is not surprising that a body of literature should emerge to reflect this.

Faced with the prospect of change, people respond in a variety of ways. Some may issue fevered warnings that things are going from bad to worse, while others may preach that Paradise is just around the corner. Science fiction has always embraced both these extremes, as well as many other alternatives in between; it has always taken the idea of change for granted.

In his history of sf, *Billion Year Spree**, Brian Aldiss plausibly identified Mary Shelley's *Frankenstein* (1818) as the first true science fiction novel. The monster in the story – created by man – symbolises many of the hopes and fears associated with the new power that science was giving the human race over nature. Other writers followed with cautionary tales of invasion or disaster, and adventure stories of the kind associated with Jules Verne which show a fascination with the world's wonders, be they natural or man-made. And at the turn of the century H. G. Wells produced his 'scientific romances' in which prescriptions for new social orders intermingled with an underlying pessimism about the actual prospects of a change for the better. Men may have had the potential to become like gods, but Wells never forgot that they had feet of clay.

Modern science fiction took shape (and acquired its name) in cheap 'pulp' magazines in the USA during the 1920s and 30s. Urged on by enthusiastic editors, poorly paid writers churned out great quantities of crude stories which nevertheless found a wide audience. These editors and writers often knew one another personally and exchanged ideas for stories. Together they succeeded in creating a genre to which almost all sf writers, fifty years on, pay some homage.

Science fiction has still not shrugged off the stigma of these humble

*Recently revised (with David Wingrove) as *Trillion Year Spree*

origins. Many people consider it vulgar and intrinsically third-rate, and in Britain, for example, it still lacks the cachet of crime fiction.

This is not entirely surprising. Classic crime fiction is a tragedy of manners, a drama played out in a clearly defined environment to set rules. It concerns the establishment of order, the use of deduction to isolate and remove from society a dangerous element. As such, it offers intellectual stimulus with the comfort of knowing the ropes. Hence it tends (in its purest form) to appeal to the conservatism in people.

Science fiction, by contrast, frequently goes out of its way to flout familiarity and familiar modes of behaviour. The last thing it expects is for things to remain the same. Its *frisson* is the shock of the new and the strange. Often it is undeniably vulgar. Even when well written, it may be rejected because its purview is the sciences rather than the humanities and hence outside the scope of what many people consider as 'culture'.

Pick a selection of sf paperbacks off the bookshelves, and the chances are that their covers will show garish renditions of spaceships, bizarre aliens, hulking robots and perhaps a scantily clad female or two. This sort of imagery plays up to the popular stereotype of science fiction as still a creature of its pulp origins, offering the equivalent of Cowboys and Indians in space or gothic horror in technological guise. And it is true that much sf does still fall into the category of unsophisticated adventure stories in which men are heroic, women winsome and vulnerable, and the baddies – be they sinister aliens, cold-hearted robots or mutant monsters – thoroughly bad.

This kind of science fiction differs from more serious forms in that its appeal lies in its being familiar and predictable. A triumphant outcome is rarely in doubt, the milieu holds few surprises, and the range of human responses is limited and pat. True imagination and inventive-ness – qualities which sf is always claiming for itself – are conspicuous by their absence. And it has to be said that these formulaic adventures are often very popular with readers. The comforts of familiarity are seductive.

More ambitious science fiction, however, seeks to challenge and provoke. It aims to upset readers' cosy assumptions, and it does so by taking them out of the world which they know and into other places and times where different rules apply. Typical themes in science fiction include time-travel and voyages to other dimensions and planets. These are ways for the reader to journey vicariously into the distant past, to other earths where history may have taken a different course, or into the future where the human race is busy colonising the universe.

Time and space know no bounds for sf writers; they can play fast and loose with the whole of creation. But although science fiction often deals in futures, it is not primarily a *prophetic* literature in the sense of offering a crystal ball through which we can glimpse what lies ahead. Instead it consists of speculations whose purpose may be cautionary, inspirational, ironic, satiric, and so on. Very few writers in the field believe that the worlds they invent will actually come into being. They may extrapolate, but that is not the same thing as prediction.

It is also worth remembering that writers are bounded by the time in which they live. Fiction of whatever nature reflects the society from which it emerges. This isn't to suggest that all science fiction is reducible to veiled comments on the here and now. It often makes a concerted effort to imagine worlds and societies as different from the present day as possible. But at the same time, sf often dates more rapidly than other kinds of fiction since its speculations are more easily overtaken by events – events which put it into immediate historical perspective. It always carries echoes of the issues and interests of the day, however obliquely.

There are many varieties of science fiction, but all are essentially about some form of 'otherness'. On this basis, it is possible to subdivide the field broadly into four categories, with the proviso that the categories are by no means mutually exclusive and may often be throughly interlinked. It contains stories dealing with:

1 Other times
2 Other worlds
3 Other beings
4 Other states of mind

Other times

'Other times' include both the future and the past. Normally, of course, the latter is the province of the historical novelist, but as far as science fiction is concerned, journeys into earlier epochs imply time-travel, either with or without a time-machine.

The idea of time-travel immediately raises many paradoxes. What if a man went back in time and killed his parents before he himself was born? What if a woman married her father before *she* was born? Better still, what if our intrepid chrononaut decided to assassinate Hitler or Napoleon or William the Conqueror, thus altering the whole course of history?

Science fiction delights in exploring such possibilities. Ray Bradbury's short story 'A Sound of Thunder' is one of the starkest and most effective demonstrations of the theme. A time-machine takes a man over sixty million years into the past. He is warned not to step off the metal path which floats just above the prehistoric landscape. But he panics when threatened by a Tyrannosaurus rex, leaves the path and inadvertently steps on a butterfly, killing it. On returning to the future he discovers that the death of the butterfly has ultimately caused a grim dictatorship to replace the democracy in which he originally lived.

Whereas historical novelists will usually aim to portray their chosen period as accurately as possible, science fiction writers who take us into the past have different fish to fry. They may indeed stick to historical fact in plunging their time-travellers into World War I, the Biblical period or the Stone Age, but the very existence of the anomalous time-traveller creates quite a different focus of interest. Something new is bound to happen, and it is just a question of when.

Often the dramatic tension arises from the clash between the ancient and the modern in the story. Michael Moorcock has used this tension to hilarious effect in his trilogy *The Dancers at the End of Time*. Jherek Carnelian arrives in Victorian London in search of his fiancée. Jherek comes from a wonderfully decadent future where the whole environment can be recreated according to an individual's whim. But although his epoch is advanced scientifically, Jherek himself is an innocent, knowing very little about the period in which he finds himself:

He struck off across the street and at that moment his ears were filled by a peculiar clacking noise, a rattling noise. He heard a shout. He looked to his left and saw a black beast emerging from the fog. Its eyes rolled, its nostrils flared.

'A horse!' he cried. 'It is a horse!'
He had often made his own, of course, but it was not the same as seeing the original.
Again the shout.
He shouted back, cheering and waving his arms.
The horse was drawing something behind it – a tall black carriage on top of which was perched a man with a whip. It was the man who was shouting.
The horse stood up on its hind legs as Jherek waved. It seemed to him that the horse was waving back to him. Strange to be greeted by a beast on one's first arrival in a century.
Then Jherek felt something strike him on the head and he fell down and to one side as the horse and carriage clattered past him and disappeared into the fog. . . .
Soon, as he raised himself to his hands and knees, he saw about a dozen men and women all like himself, dressed in period, standing in a circle around him . . . He raised the translation pill to his lips and swallowed it . . .
'Have you any idea what happened to me just then?' Jherek asked . . .

'You wos knocked darn by an 'ansom, that's wot 'appened to you, me old gonolph,' said a man in a tone of great satisfaction . . .

One of the women helped Jherek to get to his feet. She seemed a bit wrinkled and she smelt very strongly of something Jherek could not identify. Her face was covered in a variety of paints and powders.

She leered at him.

Politely Jherek leered back.

'Thank you,' he said.

'That's all right, lovey,' said the lady . . . 'Wanna warm bed for the night, do yer?' She snuggled her body up against him, adding in a murmur for his ears alone. 'It won't cost yer much. I like the looks o' you.'

'You wish to make love to me?' he said, realisation dawning. 'I'm flattered. You are very wrinkled. It would be interesting. Unfortunately, however, I am—'

'Cheek!' She dropped her arm from his. 'Bleedin' cheek! . . . '

This passage shows a delight in the kind of clash between cultures which is often at the heart of science fiction. Time-travel into the past allows many possibilities, including the discovery of long-vanished civilisations unknown to history so that writers have free scope for invention. Atlantis and Lemuria have been typical favourites in this respect.

Time-travel into the future also has a distinguished place in science fiction, notably in the work of H. G. Wells. But modern sf has largely done away with the need for an everyman of our time to visit the future so that we can see its marvels through his eyes. Nowadays writers simply present their futures from the perspectives of the actual inhabitants. This is time-travel in a more metaphorical sense.

Imagined futures cover the spectrum from Utopias, which illustrate ideal or idealised societies, to Dystopias, where things have gone horribly wrong. Utopian fiction is rare nowadays (we live in more cynical times) and it is always difficult to do well since near-perfect societies by their nature tend to lack the capacity for drama or conflict, unless a spanner can be thrown into the works (in which case the writer's aim is often an *attack* on Utopianism, as with Aldous Huxley's *Brave New World*). Nowadays writers with Utopian leanings seldom imagine that a perfect society could exist, even as a thought-experiment. Ursula LeGuin's *The Dispossessed* is a distinguished example of a flawed Utopia, which shows an attempt to create an egalitarian society based on anarchist principles; but the society falls far short of being perfect, not least because its people are very real.

Dystopias, by contrast, all too readily spring to mind, with writers taking contemporary trends and magnifying them to create societies in which the worst has happened. George Orwell's *Nineteen Eighty-Four* is a classic example, the totalitarian extremism in the novel being extrapolated from the political climate which prevailed in the years immediately after World War II. In the 1950s the Cold War led to a spate of stories about nuclear catastrophes, and Walter M. Miller's *A Canticle For Liebowitz* describes a post-holocaust Earth slowly rediscovering its technology, whose secrets have been preserved in monasteries, only to destroy itself all over again.

In the 1960s writers such as Harry Harrison and John Brunner produced grim warnings of near-future Earths swamped by overpopulation or pollution in such novels as *Make Room! Make Room!*, *Stand on Zanzibar* and *The Sheep Look Up*. In the 1970s a variety of ecocatastrophes mirrored the concern with environmental issues. The 1980s have seen something of a return to stories dealing with nuclear catastrophe, echoing the renewed fears of the dangers of the arms race. No doubt the current spectre of AIDS will soon make its presence felt in sf.

Frequently such tales of doom offer a masochistic relish for both writers and readers, no matter how seriously they may be intended; there is nothing quite like a juicy catastrophe, as long as it is vicarious. The disaster novel is a whole sub-genre in itself: writers like John Wyndham, John Christopher and J. G. Ballard are expert in their very different ways at dreaming up threats to the Earth in the form of seamonsters, comets, ice ages, floods, drought and ambulant plants.

This should not, however, suggest that science fiction always concentrates on the darker potential of our immediate future. More often we find a mixture of good and bad, and in the works of Robert Heinlein, Arthur C. Clarke, Frederik Pohl and many others, the future is frequently seen as a place abrim with potential for the enterprising or the fortunate. Or, for satirists like Robert Sheckley, Kurt Vonnegut Jr, and John Sladek, it may be filled with the absurdities of our own culture, taken to extremes, as in Vonnegut's 'Harrison Bergeron', where the USA of a hundred years hence has a Handicapper General to ensure that everyone is forcibly made as equal as possible. In feminist sf, a relatively new but vigorous branch of sf, the future may show women totally oppressed by men, or, conversely, there being no men at all. More recently, the widespread arrival of computer technology has been absorbed, and William Gibson's *Neuromancer* is a vivid portrayal of a future dominated by multi-national corporations and user-friendly machines in run-down cities. It is worth noting here that much sf has an urban setting since it is in cities that new technologies and new social orders tend to emerge.

In this section we have restricted ourselves to the future on Earth, but of course science fiction has always assumed that the human race will spread outwards into the solar system and other worlds beyond.

Other worlds

'To boldly go where no man has gone before', in the words of the 1960s TV series *Star Trek*, has long been a clarion call to sf. Humans have been voyaging fictionally to other worlds for centuries, and the genre has made such trips one of its specialities.

Before the 20th century, other worlds were often found in remote corners of the Earth, or even at the Earth's core. Nowadays this sort of thing is seen as anachronistic (unless the writer can come up with a completely new angle on the notion) since the Earth is too well explored. Sub-atomic worlds were also envisaged, based on the idea (now known to be erroneous) that atoms were just like miniature solar systems. Or shrunken explorers might find life in a drop of water, perhaps an entire civilisation. In Isaac Asimov's *Fantastic Voyage* they enter the human body itself.

Generally, though, miniature worlds have always been much less popular than other planets. The Moon and our nearest neighbours Mars and Venus have long been favourite fictional landscapes with writers as varied as Wells, Edgar Rice Burroughs, Robert Heinlein, Arthur C. Clarke and many others. If the Moon was usually shown as sterile and airless, Mars was often portrayed as a world of canals and civilisations, Venus as a hot and/or rainy place beneath its dense clouds. Mercury and the outer planets have featured less regularly, but all still occur in sf.

Science fiction is sometimes divided into 'hard' and 'soft' sf, loose terms which broadly separate writers who strive for a conspicuous show of scientific accuracy from those more concerned with social and metaphorical possibilities and never mind the nuts and bolts of the matter. These different approaches are a matter of taste and temperament, and each has its own virtues. Often it is in stories centred on other planets that the contrast between the two approaches can best be seen. A romantically inclined writer such as Ray Bradbury can, in *The Martian Chronicles*, describe a Mars which is hopelessly out of date astronomically but which still possesses symbolic and dramatic power. By contrast, Arthur C. Clarke, in his story 'A Meeting With Medusa', takes the latest information on the nature of Jupiter to describe life-forms which might exist in its dense turbulent atmosphere. More recently, science fiction, in becoming more self-conscious, has also become more self-referential, with writers often acknowledging the genre's past, as in *Icehenge* by Kim Stanley Robinson, where echoes of the Mars of Bradbury are combined with a modern awareness of the planet's nature.

Beyond the Solar System lie countless other suns, and, presumably, planets orbiting them. But now we encounter the problem of distance.

A spaceship which could travel at the speed of light would take five and a half hours to reach the edge of the Solar System from the Sun. But to reach the next star would take over four years; and to cross our galaxy would take a hundred thousand years. Beyond this lie other galaxies, stretching to the edges of the universe.

Modern science places the speed of light as an upper limit on how fast any object can travel. Thus any writer wishing to treat seriously the exploration of other star-systems is immediately faced with problems of time-scale. Various means have been used to overcome this.

The simplest is the 'faster-than-light' drive, which makes the assumption that in the future some means *will* be found of overcoming the light/speed barrier, thus solving the problem at a stroke. Or writers may invoke the related idea of 'hyperspace', a kind of extra dimension where distance is reduced to zero so that spacecraft entering hyperspace can cover vast distances in no time at all. On a similar basis, teleportation and matter transmission assume instantaneous travel between places.

Ideas like hyperspace and matter transmission have no strict scientific basis, but they are legitimate sf notions which carry the implication that future science and technology have made breakthroughs considered impossible in our time. Often it is the speculations of scientists themselves which give sf writers their notions: when black holes were postulated by theoretical astronomers, they soon became a popular feature in stories, typically being used as yet another means for starships to plunge through into other parts of the universe or into other universes entirely. The idea that writers should slavishly be bound by known physics is a narrow one; *anything* may be invented, providing that it seems scientifically feasible.

Many writers do, however, prefer to stick to the rules as we know them and have devised equally ingenious means of taking their starships across the gulfs of space. The theory of relativity tells us that for an object travelling at very high speeds, time actually slows down relative to the universe outside it so that it is in fact possible for a starship to cover great distances in the course of the crew's lifetime while centuries or millennia may pass on Earth.

Writers have enjoyed playing with the consequences of this 'time-dilation' effect. The classic situation is that of two twins, one of whom travels out into space at high speed, eventually returning to find that his Earth-bound brother is old while he himself remains relatively young. In *Tau Zero*, Poul Anderson has an out-of-control starship constantly accelerating at close to the speed of light so that time slows practically to a standstill for the crew while outside the whole universe is ageing rapidly. It is hard to imagine a more awesome idea than this, and it is quintessentially science-fictional.

Alternatively, writers may have their starship crews put into 'suspended animation' – a deep sleep with their bodily processes frozen for the duration of the voyage. Or there's the 'generation' starship, in which space voyages lasting centuries or longer are completed by the descendants of the original crew, children being born and raised on board the ship, later to take over its running when they reach adulthood. Such ships are effectively worlds within themselves. A related idea is the artificial habitat, a sphere or cylinder or hollowed asteroid with a whole environment inside it to allow its inhabitants to survive in space indefinitely. On an even larger scale, Larry Niven in *Ringworld* and Bob Shaw in *Orbitsville* respectively described stars surrounded by an enormous ring and a shell of material, the inhabitants living on their inner surfaces.

Alien planets themselves provide near endless scope for the enterprising writer: they can be fashioned in almost any image. Statistically the chances of finding habitable planets orbiting other stars may be slim, but in science fiction such worlds abound, a reflection of our desire to colonise the universe and our hope that at least parts of it will be friendly.

Often such planets come complete with advanced alien species, but aliens will be considered under 'Other beings'. Human explorers can face many other dangers such as hostile climates, oppressive gravities, lethal animal or vegetable or mineral life, a toxic atmosphere, or the machinations of other humans. 'Terraforming' involves deliberately redesigning a planet so that humans can live there. Sometimes the planet may exist simply as an exotic locale for colourful adventures, as in much of Jack Vance's work; or it may be just a particle in one of the Galactic Empires so beloved of sf.

It was in Frank Herbert's *Dune* that the alien planet really took centre stage in science fiction. Herbert's detailed evocation of the desert world Arrakis, with its huge sandworms and its nomadic Fremen, created a continuing trend for 'world-building' novels in which authors expressly set out to create as a complete a picture of another planet as possible:

> Desert hawks, carrion-eaters in this land as were most wild creatures, began to circle over him. Kynes saw a shadow pass near his hand, forced his head farther around to look upward. The birds were a blurred patch on silver-blue sky – distant flecks of soot floating above him . . .
> 'We are generalists,' his father said. 'You can't draw neat lines around planet-wide problems. Planetology is a cut-and-fit science.'
> *What's he trying to tell me?* Kynes wondered. *Is there something I failed to see?*
> His cheek slumped back against the hot sand, and he smelled the burned rock odour beneath the pre-spice gases.

This is a fairly unremarkable passage in the context of the book as a whole, but in a brief space Herbert evokes colour, shade, sound, thought, touch and smell in order to bring the scene alive.

With the entire universe as a potential backdrop, science fiction is often spoiled for choice. At one extreme is space opera (the term is used either fondly or pejoratively, according to inclination), typified by the popular 'Lensman' series of E. E. 'Doc' Smith, in which the good Arisians battle continually against the evil Eddorians. By contrast, Olaf Stapledon's visions of the future development of the human race as outlined in *First and Last Men* and *Star Maker* owe nothing to genre sf and display a breadth of imagination which is awesome in all senses of the word.

There is one further category of other world: that which can't be reached by travel through time or space in the accepted sense but which lies in another 'dimension', perhaps coexistent with our own Earth. These are parallel worlds, and they may be quite different from our own or quite similar except for one or two crucial historical changes, in which case they qualify as 'alternate Earths'.

Parallel worlds offer similar scope to other planets in that they may take any form the author chooses. In some respects they offer more, Isaac Asimov's *The Gods Themselves* and Bob Shaw's *A Wreath of Stars* presenting universes in which the actual laws of nature are different. In Keith Laumer's 'Worlds of the Imperium' they simply provide colourful locales for ingenious adventures. In Brian Aldiss's *Report on Probability A*, where observers from different realities study one another, they bring science fiction close in its concerns to post-modernist fiction in which the author's influence in the shaping of the story is explicitly acknowledged in the text.

Alternate Earths tend to be similar to our own, writers usually assuming that a single point of historical divergence gave rise to a different world. In Ward Moore's *Bring the Jubilee* the Confederate States won the American Civil War; in Philip K. Dick's *The Man in the High Castle* an America defeated in World War II is divided into German and Japanese zones; in Keith Roberts's *Pavane* the English Reformation petered out as a result of the assassination of Elizabeth I and the Industrial Revolution never happened. Often alternate Earths are less advanced and less pleasant places than our own, though in *A Transatlantic Tunnel, Hurrah!* Harry Harrison celebrates a world in which the USA happily remains a colony of the still-thriving British Empire. Other worlds, and in particular other Earths, offer a kind of warped mirror which reflects the unrealised potentials of our own history.

Other beings

If space travel and voyages to distant planets show sf's extrovert side, other beings often allow an introspective approach. As other worlds reflect our own society, so other beings may reflect ourselves. Science fiction has three favourite types: altered humans, artificial humans and aliens.

In much early sf, altered humans arise as the result of mutation, rather simplistically perceived as the effect of radiation on the human form which induces physiological changes. The resulting mutants were often shambling sub-humans – or, alternatively, they might gain new physical or mental powers (typically extra-sensory perception). The degenerate mutant brings out the beast in us, and it often results from the aftermath of nuclear war, so that not only is civilisation destroyed but also the mental capacities which gave rise to it.

Superhumans, by contrast, may symbolise our god-like potential, though they may be feared because they imply the obsolescence of ordinary human beings. Often they arise as the next step in evolution. Books such as Theodore Sturgeon's *More Than Human*, Robert Heinlein's *Stranger in a Strange Land* and many of Ian Watson's novels, all deal in various ways with the emergence of new forms of human beings and new states of existence. Single individuals may become new Messiahs, or groups may cease to be individuals at all and fuse into some form of cosmic or gestalt mind.

Closely associated with the superhuman is the immortal (or the very long-lived) human. Again, science fiction has shown mixed feelings on the subject, some writers seeing long life as desirable, others as disastrous for the human spirit. Infertility is frequently the price paid for immortality in sf (which coincidentally pays homage to the modern biological theory that the survival value of a species depends on the propagation of genes through offspring rather than the well-being of specific individuals). Robert Silverberg, a writer very preoccupied with death and various means of avoiding it, has addressed the question of extended life in much of his fiction, notably 'Born with the Dead' and *The Book of Skulls*.

Another way in which altered humans may arise is through *design* rather than accident. A typical example would be 'pantropy', the reverse of terraforming, whereby humans are genetically engineered so that they can live unaided on hostile planets. Frederik Pohl's *Man Plus* treats the theme with both biological and psychological plausibility.

For a while the idea of 'cloning' was popular in sf, this being a non-sexual method of producing offspring identical to a single parent. Ursula Le Guin's 'Nine Lives' and Kate Wilhelm's *Where Late the Sweet Birds Sang* involve clones, and Richard Cowper's *Clone* is a more jocular variation on the theme. In James Tiptree Jr's 'Houston, Houston, Do You Read?' cloning becomes a plot device for eliminating men by making them reproductively redundant.

Artificial humans have long been popular in sf, most obviously in the form of the robot. At first robots were shown not only as servants of humans, but also as their menacers, reflecting a period when people were distinctly ambivalent about the benefits of increasing automation. In 1940 Isaac Asimov codified his three laws of robotics, which tended to domesticate the robot. Later robots were used for comic or ironic effect, with Robert Silverberg's 'Good News from the Vatican' featuring the election of the first robot pope. Barrington Bayley in *Soul of the Robot* and John Sladek in *Roderick* present robots who are more humane than many humans around them.

The android is a more sophisticated development of the robot, the term usually taken to mean an artificial creature with a much stronger resemblance to a human being, even to the point where the two cannot be distinguished. If the mad robot symbolises technology run rampant, then the mad android often represents ourselves turned into machines. Philip K. Dick was perennially fascinated by humans and machines made in an exact human image. Many of his stories deal with questions of identity and reality, frequently with reference to constructs which are perfect replicas of humans or animals – as, for example, in *Do Androids Dream of Electric Sheep?* (later filmed as *Blade Runner*). In this respect he is a thoroughly modern writer, addressing one of the major concerns of our time, the question of what is real and reliable.

Mention must also be made of 'cyborgs', a contraction of 'cybernetic organisms', implying hybrids of the human and the mechanical. Computers, too, are often perceived as artificial humans (though not humanoid in shape) who may surprise us either by transcending their programming or by blind mechanical determinism. The latter features in 'Computers Don't Argue' by Gordon R. Dickson a malfunctioning system which eventually condemns to death the hapless man who has borrowed the library book *Kidnapped* by Robert Louis Stevenson. These days computers have largely taken the place of robots as the symbol of our fear of the machine.

The alien is another central figure in sf. Ever since the pulp magazines flourished they have been cavorting through the pages of stories in an array of guises from the sublime to the ridiculous. The alien represents the most diametrically opposed form of otherness to the human, and it affords immense scope for invention.

Two essential forms of alien are found in science fiction: the humanoid and the rest. Humanoid aliens are often favoured precisely because they are similar to us, allowing us to meet them on roughly equal terms, for whatever purpose. They tend to live on planets similar to Earth, with a bearable gravity and a breathable air so that some form of discourse between the two races is possible. Implicitly they suggest that biological evolution on other worlds has taken a parallel course to that on Earth.

Of course, as in much science fiction, these are usually matters of dramatic convenience rather than considered decisions based on scientific principles. But modern sf has become more conscious of the symbolism of the humanoid alien, of its potential as a form of *alter ego* to the human. Many of Ursula Le Guin's novels feature humanoid races descended from a common stock, thus making our sense of identification more potent and hence more unnerving in a novel such as *The Left Hand of Darkness*, which features a human envoy on a world whose inhabitants are sexually neuter for much of the time but then become male or female during a fertile period called 'kemmer'. The envoy, a man, befriends a native called Estraven, whom he thinks of as 'he' until the two of them are isolated together for a period:

> We were both silent for a little, and then he looked at me with a direct, gentle gaze. His face in the reddish light was as soft, as vulnerable, as remote as the face of a woman who looks at you out of her thoughts and does not speak.
> And I saw then again, and for good, what I had always been afraid to see, and had pretended not to see in him: that he was a woman as well as a man . . .
> He explained, stiffly and simply, that he was in kemmer and had been trying to avoid me, insofar as one of us could avoid the other. 'I must not touch you,' he said, with extreme constraint; saying that he looked away.

The temptation should, however, be resisted to see all aliens as altered images of humans. Often writers seek to shock or disturb by making them as weird as possible. And Michael Bishop's careful evocations of alien societies in novels such as *A Funeral for the Eyes of Fire* and *Transfigurations* read like exercises in speculative anthropology.

Things were simpler in the early days of the pulps. Aliens were often bug-eyed monsters, as mean and nasty as the basest human. If evil, they were often based on creatures repugnant to most of us, such as insects or reptiles; if sympathetic, they tended to be rather pet-like, resembling birds or cats or cuddly bears. Later more sophisticated models were used, giving rise to alien societies based on the behaviour of bees or dolphins or ants. In theory, there is no reason to suppose that intelligent life elsewhere in the universe must resemble our own. In *The Black Cloud* the astronomer Fred Hoyle invents a completely inorganic intelligence in the form of a cloud of gases which has formed in space and survives by surrounding stars to warm itself. In Stanislaw Lem's *Solaris* the alien being takes the form of a sentient ocean, and in the same writer's *The Invincible* a team of human explorers on another planet encounters a range of bizarre phenomena which cannot be understood but which are obviously the product of some kind of intelligence. Here we are far away from the cosy humanoid alien who is not so very different from us. True aliens may be so strange that we can never hope to communicate with them.

Other states of mind

Science fiction is often perceived as dealing almost exclusively with external worlds, yet it has always shown a great interest in the mental aptitudes of human beings as well as the universe which they inhabit. Stories of people with paranormal powers abound, with telepaths (people who can mind-read and broadcast their thoughts) being perhaps the most popular. Precognition, the ability to see into the future, is another favourite, as are more active talents such as the ability to move objects with the mind (telekinesis) or to move instantaneously through space (teleportation).

Such gifts may be desirable (as in Alfred Bester's *Tiger! Tiger!*, where teleportation is a technique that can be learned) or thoroughly terrifying, as in Jerome Bixby's 'It's A *Good* Life', where a monstrous child with paranormal powers transports a whole community into limbo and forces its inhabitants to attend to his every whim on pain of gruesome death. Robert Silverberg's *Dying Inside* is a sensitive portrait of a telepath who is gradually *losing* his powers, a process which is seen to have mixed blessings.

In 1962 J. G. Ballard coined the term 'inner space' to describe the kind of sf which deals with the realm of psychological experience and its relationship to the external world. Ballard's own work shows an obsessive preoccupation with the effects of modern society on the human mind. He often uses the disaster novel as a framework, but his protagonists embrace the catastrophe rather than trying to fight it as tradition demands; their prime motive is to discover pattern and meaning from the landscape itself. So we see new forms of consciousness emerging in response to changed conditions.

Ian Watson has also shown an abiding concern with the mental potential of the human race. Much of his work involves human beings transcending their ordinary mental capacities to reach higher forms of consciousness and states of being. Frequently these processes have the quality of religious revelation. In Richard Cowper's work, people often discover how to harness mental powers which are only fleetingly expressed in ordinary life – these offer new channels of communication between individuals and sometimes access to other worlds, as in 'The White Bird of Kinship' series.

The idea of reaching or even creating other realities through the mind is also found in such novels as Christopher Priest's *Inverted World* and *The Affirmation*, and Iain Banks's *The Bridge*. Here we encounter realities which are seen to take their shape through the will of one or many individuals rather than necessarily having an objective existence. Once again this kind of sf offers a comment on the actual process of creating fiction itself.

Drugs or other agents may be used to create new states of mind, as in Thomas M. Disch's *Camp Concentration*, where a man is infected with a mutated form of syphilis which turns him into a genius. In Philip K. Dick's work, drugs may or may not be used to make the mundane world dissolve into something quite different. Dick's protagonists often undergo mental experiences similar to psychotics, but with the difference that the fantasies and illusions are often shown to be objectively real. Appearances can never be trusted in Dick's world, as a passage from an early novel, *Time Out of Joint*, demonstrates. A man walks up to a soft-drink stand in an ordinary suburban setting:

> 'Got any beer?' he said. His voice sounded funny. Thin and remote. The counter man in white apron and cap stared at him, stared and did not move. Nothing happened. No sound, anywhere. Kids, cars, the wind; it all shut off.
>
> The fifty-cent piece fell away, down through the wood, sinking. It vanished ...
>
> The soft-drink stand fell into bits. Molecules. He saw the molecules, colourless, without qualities, that made it up. Then he saw through, into the space beyond it, he saw the hill behind, the trees and sky. He saw the soft-drink stand go out of existence, along with the counter man, the cash register, the big dispenser of orange drink, the taps for Coke and root beer, the ice-chests of bottles, the hot dog broiler, the jars of mustard, the shelves of cones, the row of heavy round metal lids under which were the different ice creams.
>
> In its place was a slip of paper. He reached out his hand and took hold of the slip of paper. On it was printing, block letters.
>
> SOFT-DRINK STAND

In *Voyage to Arcturus* David Lindsay has a character transported to another planet whose body and perceptions change so that he is able to see new colours, sense emotions and so on. Synaesthesia – where the senses become jumbled so that sound may be smelt, colours tasted,

etc. – has also been used, most notably by Alfred Bester in *Tiger! Tiger!*
Non-human forms of consciousness have increasingly featured in sf,
from the sentient whales of Ian Watson's *The Jonah Kit* to the aliens
who coexist throughout time in Kurt Vonnegut Jr's *Sirens of Titan* and
Slaughterhouse Five. Robert Silverberg's 'Passengers' chillingly portrays
disembodied aliens who invade human 'hosts', temporarily blotting
out their memories and using them to commit depraved acts.

As other societies and other worlds may offer a glimpse of the
possible environments which we might create around us, so other
states of mind may show our potential for altering ourselves and our
conception of the universe. Both these concerns are absolutely central
to the nature of science fiction.

This hasty canter through the field of sf cannot hope to cover the
whole ground, but it does at least show something of its extent. More
than any other literature, science fiction takes whole universes and the
whole of time as its source material. If it has a single underlying
assumption, it's that anything is possible – or at least imaginable.

2
Ideas

Science fiction is frequently described as 'a literature of ideas', as if to imply that it has a monopoly on them and that all other kinds of fiction are concerned with something else.

Similarly, one of the questions most often asked of its writers is 'Where do you get your ideas?' This is actually a difficult question to answer satisfactorily because there is no single and simple method. It also assumes that everyone agrees on what is meant by 'ideas'. Let us pin down the meaning with regard to sf.

Idea versus theme

Isaac Asimov's well-known story 'Nightfall' is set on another planet which orbits several other suns so that night falls only once every two thousand years during an eclipse. The experience of darkness drives the inhabitants mad, so that they destroy the civilisation over and over again. The only knowledge of past disasters remains in garbled form in the 'Book of Revelation' of The Cultists, a religious sect. The story itself deals with the discovery by scientists that The Cultists' prophecies are based on astronomical facts, and that another eclipse is imminent. Preparations are made to ensure that some people will survive with their sanity intact, but The Cultists, hating what they see as interference with nature, destroy one of the sanctuaries which has been prepared against the catastrophe.

Now what is this story actually about? It is about the dangers of blind superstition and the virtues of the scientific method. But a reader asking Isaac Asimov where he got the idea for 'Nightfall' is likely to mean 'Where did you get the idea of a planet where night never falls?' In science fiction, ideas tend to mean things or situations with novelty value.

The fact that ideas (or situations with novelty value) are highly prized in sf can have its dangers – especially for new writers. One of the exciting things about first discovering sf is that readers are suddenly confronted with exotic places and notions and beings. If they have the urge to write themselves, they tend to want to recreate that feeling of excitement by producing stories which also feature exotic places and notions and things. Too often this leads them to concentrate on trying to invent new gimmicks or striking situations *as an end in itself.* They overrate novelty value at the expense of *theme* − what statement the story is actually making about larger issues. And in fact, they usually fail even on that score. With their limited exposure to sf, they are surprised to discover that what seems like a fresh idea or a cunning variation on a classic situation frequently proves to be old hat.

A point worth stressing is that in science fiction, as in all other forms of literature, *originality is actually in short supply.* New ideas in a science-fictional sense tend to crop up only rarely, even for writers with a penchant for them. An emphasis on novelty value is one best resisted unless you happen to have a very distinctive imagination. More important is to write about what matters to you − in other words to produce stories which develop from your own interests in life. The best stories usually have a strong theme − they are about something more than clever notions or flashy effects.

Of course, the theme of a story is often obvious only after it has been written, and it is true that much science fiction comes into existence because the writer gets a good idea rather than wants to make a particular statement. On a conscious level, a story may be written purely for entertainment, in which case the writer's subconscious supplies the theme. With 'Nightfall' it is likely that the story originated from the notion of a planet where night never falls. But the story which emerged from this premise − a story praising scientists and condemning religious fanaticism − is reflective of Isaac Asimov's underlying attitudes and interests. Without these, there would have been no story at all.

Voice

Stories which have a strong theme illustrate something of the author, however obliquely. This is what is often meant by *voice.* Voice is what gives fiction its personality; it is the author's world-view coming through. Often it is missing in beginners because they have yet to shake off the influence of other writers. Producing stories after the fashion of your favourite author is usually frowned upon, but to begin with it may be a necessary stage of development. Most often, of course, such mimicry is not done consciously, but whether deliberate or not, it's a practice that is only likely to be harmful if persisted in, in which case it can stifle the author's own individuality.

Being true to your own interests applies even if you simply wish to produce efficient entertainment which does not aspire to having any particular moral or personal significance. The best entertainers are those whose work is filled with their desire to entertain. Robert Heinlein is often cited as someone with a very hard-nosed and businesslike approach to sf, but he is also a writer of passionate convictions whose personality shows strongly in his work. In the long term, writers are better advised to write about what fascinates them rather than trying to chase an audience; if they do it well, an audience will find them.

Generating ideas

'Where do you get your ideas?' Writers are usually asked this question in the hope that they will reveal a specific technique for doing so. But unlike many other aspects of writing, the generation of ideas can't be learned from others; it can only be encouraged in yourself. At the risk of stating the obvious, ideas come from the imagination, and that imagination is in turn the product of the sum total of an individual's life experiences.

Would-be writers who feel deficient in ideas can take practical steps to cultivate their imaginations. A common fallacy is that writers should lead exciting and colourful lives, joining safaris or taking canoes up the Limpopo at every opportunity. No doubt such experiences are valuable (and it is an interesting fact that many well-known sf writers such as Brian Aldiss, J. G. Ballard and Arthur C. Clarke have all spent periods living overseas in cultures quite different from their own) but in themselves they actually have very little to do with the business of creating fiction. *All* experiences, however outwardly dull, may stimulate the mind.

Writers need to cultivate an observant attitude and an interest in other people and things. The prospective science fiction writer tends to be particularly fascinated by the effects of change on people and institutions, by new inventions, different life-styles, emerging technologies, and so on. In the modern world change usually has its roots in scientific developments, so an interest in these matters is important. It's not necessary to be a science graduate in order to write sf, but a basic scientific literacy and a healthy curiosity about social and technological possibilities is necessary since these lie at the heart of all the best sf.

Assuming that you have the appropriate curiosity about such matters, then the best way to cultivate your imagination is to *feed your head*. Direct experience does this automatically, of course, but books, radio, television and cinema can all provide useful input. Yet selectivity is important, especially in what you read. Many new writers tend to read science fiction exclusively, and this is often a big mistake. It is useful to be familiar with the field before trying to write sf yourself – this can reduce the danger of rehashing tired old storylines – but to read nothing else is to risk having your imagination conditioned by the genre. It becomes hard to find a fresh approach if you are constantly filling your head with other writers' stories. Many successful sf authors actually read very little science fiction; their inspiration comes from outside the field, and their imagination remains fresh precisely because of this.

The more diverse your reading, the better. Magazines such as *New Scientist* and *Scientific American* can be valuable sources of ideas since they're always reporting what's happening at the cutting edge of science and technology. As nothing dates more quickly than old sf ideas, it is important to keep abreast of new developments. But it is equally important to be aware of the social context in which these developments are occurring, of trends in everything from politics to popular culture, art to architecture, medicine to music. So read a good newspaper and any other magazines, journals and non-fiction books that take your fancy. Specific subjects can be useful for specific stories. For example, the writer who wishes to create a weird and convincing alien society might do well to read some anthropology in order to get ideas on how other cultures have lived.

Radio, television and cinema can also feed the mind. Listening to radio drama, for example, may stimulate the ability to visualise scenes or produce good dialogue. A natural history programme on television might inspire you to create the landscape of an alien planet or the strange creatures which inhabit it. Even soap opera and advertisements can be inspirational, highlighting the absurdities of our own society which can then be exaggerated for comic or ironic effect. Cinema may provide striking images and a wide-screen sense of scope.

But above all, *read* widely, for reading is the most intimate and individual form of intellectual stimulus. As well as non-fiction, it is helpful to read all kinds of good literature. Sometimes there is an inverted snobbery in sf circles towards what is termed 'mainstream literature', meaning general non-category fiction. It is often dismissed as irrelevant to sf, mere doodlings with kitchen-sink drama as opposed to the cosmic scope of science fiction. But this prejudice is both ignorant and foolish. Irrespective of subject matter, reading authors who produce good prose, create strong characters and bring intelligence and sensitivity to their stories is always an enriching experience.

To repeat: originality is actually in short supply in science fiction, and writers stand more chance of bringing something new to the field if they have other interests and have read widely outside it.

Idea into story

Obviously some sort of idea is necessary as the starting-point for a story. But ideas aren't necessarily specific notions or inventions. Writers may start with a set of characters who intrigue them or a particular situation which has fired their imagination. A story may then begin to emerge from these. It may develop naturally, and without the writer having any clear plan of where it is heading as it is being written. Some writers are only able to work in this way, being motivated by the excitement of discovering their story as they go along. Others prefer to plan a story beforehand, either roughly or in great detail.

Both approaches have their dangers. Letting the story emerge naturally entails the risk of it becoming shapeless and requires both trust in your own instincts and a good sense of dramatic proportion. Planning a story beforehand may tend to make it schematic and lacking in spontaneity unless the writer is able to let the story dictate its own terms should the plan begin to stifle it. Sometimes different stories require different approaches, or a combination of the two.

A story is a series of incidents which illustrates an idea (in its loosest sense) in a dramatic context. Stories are sometimes subdivided into four parts:

1   Opening
2   Development
3   Climax
4   Resolution

The *opening* is obviously the reader's introduction to the story, and it should describe a situation which is intriguing in some way so that there is an immediate urge to read on. The *development*, usually the longest part of the story, will be designed to clarify the setting and complicate the plot. In other words, it reveals more of the world in which the story takes place and has a series of incidents with dramatic repercussions leading up to the *climax*. The climax is the critical point in the story at which whatever conflict is taking place reaches its peak. This conflict may vary from physical to psychological activity, so that a climax could involve a battle or a sudden realisation which leads on to some kind of transformation, made either explicit or left implicit in the *resolution*.

This is, of course, a very dry and schematic view of a story. It does describe a satisfying dramatic structure, but it shouldn't be interpreted too literally. For example, stories aren't always linear in time, so that an opening may be followed by a flashback to earlier events. There may be more than one climax (in novels there will probably be several) or there might be an ending in which nothing is obviously resolved. Slavish or simplistic adherence to any formula will result in mechanical plots. Writing isn't a science, and so its rules are always flexible; the principles of good craftsmanship should never be allowed to stifle spontaneity.

How does a story emerge from an idea? Often the two are intimately connected. Here's Bob Shaw, writing in the magazine *Vector* about the genesis of his novel, *The Ragged Astronauts*:

> For many years I had a yearning to write a story featuring verticality ... and my compulsion was to deal in thousands of miles ... I was beginning to wonder if it would ever be possible to put a handle on the idea, then one day while idly glancing through an atlas of the solar system I noted the peculiar relationship between Pluto and its single moon, Charon. The two are quite similar in size, and Charon revolves around Pluto at a surface-to-surface distance of only 15,000 kilometres ... Furthermore, Charon hangs above the same spot on Pluto – an awe-inspiring spectacle for the notional inhabitants of either body.
>
> That was it!
>
> I had seen those facts on paper a few times previously, but not until this occasion did I experience that turmoil at the centre of the being which is often referred to as inspiration. That's the way it works. When you're in the market for an idea, the conscious mind seems to put a requisition slip in to the subconscious, a search begins and – sooner or later – *bingo*!
>
> In that single moment I saw the universe of *The Ragged Astronauts* in its entirety, though without details as yet – the sister worlds of Land and Overland, each hanging at a fixed point in the other's sky, looming, beckoning, occupying a large portion of the heavens, occulting the sun every day, producing a diurnal cycle of foreday, littlenight, aftday, forenight, deepnight, aftnight ...
>
> And that was where the real work of planning the book began.
>
> Built into the original inspiration was the idea of a journey from Land to Overland, but it had to be an *epic* journey. In other words, it had to be accomplished by people whose science was not quite up to it. That premise fixed the inhabitants of Land at a level of technology roughly equal to 16th century Europe. And brought with it the first major problem.
>
> Even when assisted by low gravity, the voyagers would be unequal to the task of crossing an interplanetary vacuum, so – not without qualms – I took the steps of enveloping both worlds in a common atmosphere ... I could visualise [readers] with astronomical knowledge shaking their heads at the thought of small worlds having atmospheres thousands of miles deep.

But when you're a professional sf writer, you don't abandon a cherished idea without a fight – so I moved my sister planets into a different universe where some of the laws of physics differ from ours. When writing *The Ragged Astronauts* I didn't go into detail about the differences ... but suffice it to say that the differences are exactly those required to make possible all the things I wanted to be possible in the story. When you create a fictional universe you become a microcosmic god – and half the fun of it is taking advantage of the system by laying down your own laws and issuing your own set of commandments ...

So far, so good. I had given myself an environment with thousands of miles of vertical air space to work with or within. I had the prospect of being able to write chapter after chapter of pure verticality – but verticality is meaningless without horizontality, which in this context means a world and its people and their history.

Bob Shaw then goes on to describe some of the problems he encountered in creating a convincing world, but it is clear from the quote above that a central part of the story – an epic journey between two planets – presented itself to him as a means of dramatising *verticality*. Thus, from an idea which in its purest form is an abstract noun, he begins the process of inventing another entire universe. This process involves a combination of sheer inspiration and a healthy amount of that mental perspiration which is always required to make a piece of fiction convincing on its own terms.

Internal consistency

Another essential attribute of good sf arises from the discussion above – internal consistency. Writers may invent whatever they wish in a story, but readers must feel that there is an underlying rationale for it. What this means in practice is that writers must think through the implications of their ideas as thoroughly as possible so that there are no loopholes or inconsistencies. It is not necessary to *explain* everything in the story, but it is important to convince readers that an explanation is possible. In other words, they need to feel that the writer knows how the whole of a fictional universe operates, even if only a fraction of it is shown in a story. Internal consistency is, of course, necessary in all sorts of fiction, but it is even more important in sf precisely because anything may be invented at the outset. Readers will readily accept different ground-rules in a story (they will probably delight in them), but they will then expect the writer to stick by them throughout.

Short story or novel?

The short story and the novel represent the two extremes in length of fiction – anything from a paragraph to several hundred pages or more. Most writers prefer to work on a modest scale to begin with (though seldom as modest as a paragraph!) and the sf writer has an advantage in this respect since the short story remains in vigorous health. Indeed, it has been argued that it represents the ideal vehicle for sf, allowing for the expression of ideas in their purest form. Practically all the best-known writers in the field began by publishing short work in the kind of sf magazines which still exist today.

In short stories there is obviously less scope for developing ideas and characters than with the novel, but the form does have its advantages. In practical terms, the writer is able to complete a story in a matter of days or weeks rather than the months or years it might take to finish a novel. Mistakes and failed experiments also tend to be less dispiriting if they are six-thousand rather than sixty-thousand-word failures. Ideally short stories will encourage conciseness and tight (though not cramped) plotting.

With a novel it is harder to maintain a consistency of purpose and to prevent the story from going entirely out of control or running into a dead-end or simply collapsing through creative exhaustion. Even if the writer doggedly ploughs on to the bitter end, the result may be a ramble with no thematic or dramatic unity. Of course the novel does allow writers the leisure to explore setting and character in greater depth, and it does allow for more dramatic variety. Writers at ease with the short story sometimes find novels difficult, and vice versa. As with the sprint and the marathon, they both require creative fitness but different kinds of mental stamina.

The novel is usually vaguely defined as a 'book-length' work, the short story as anything up to twenty or thirty pages, sometimes more. But in science fiction, a field which loves categories, precise demarcations have been made between fictions of differing lengths. In the annual Hugo and Nebula Awards, which are presented for the best sf of a given year, four categories are used for fiction:

1   The short story (under 7,500 words)
2   The novelette (7,500 to 17,500 words)
3   The novella (17,500 to 40,000 words)
4   The novel (over 40,000 words)

To translate these into typescript pages, let us assume a writer uses double-spacing (that is, a space equivalent to a typed line between each line) with good margins and so gets, say, twenty-eight lines on a page with an average of eleven words per line. Rounded off, that is three hundred words on a page. So a short story would represent anything up to 25 typescript pages, a novelette 25 to about 60 pages, a novella 60 to 133 pages, and a novel anything longer than this.

These figures are quoted so that the writer has some idea of what is meant by the four categories. A story should always dictate its own length, and categories are something that are imposed on it after it is written.

The fix-up

There is one final class of story which seems to be a particular speciality of science fiction and which has been rather inelegantly termed the 'fix-up'. This is a kind of hybrid between the short story and the novel. It comprises a series of linked stories which may be complete in themselves but which add up to something larger — the portrait of a world seen through the eyes of different characters, perhaps, or, conversely, the adventures of an individual in different places. The stories often appear independently of one another, and only later are collected into a novel-length volume. A 'fix-up' often arises because the author comes up with a setting or character in one story which merits further development in others.

Fix-ups can therefore be a convenient way for the writer of short stories to produce a novel-length work with some dramatic unity. Sometimes short stories are expressly designed as individual chapters of a novel. Many well-known sf books were first published in self-contained parts, for example Isaac Asimov's *Foundation*, Walter M. Miller's *A Canticle for Liebowitz*, Keith Roberts' *Pavane* and Joe Haldeman's *The Forever War*. The advantages are obvious — a work with the dimensions of a novel can be built up in manageable sections. The danger is that the final result may be less than the sum of its parts, an assemblage which is too fragmented to have a larger unity.

Great clichés of science fiction

Before turning to the basic elements of story-telling, it is worth mentioning a few situations and notions which the new writer would be wise to avoid because they and their variations have been overworked in the field:

Adam and Eve revisited   A man wanders across a ravaged landscape, the only person alive after a nuclear war. Then, among the rubble, he hears a voice. Digging frantically, he uncovers a woman. She is beautiful, adores him on sight. Immediately they fall in love. 'The human race will rise again from us,' he tells her. 'We will be the new Adam and the new Eve.' Good grief, thinks the reader, not *that* old turkey.

A planet called Htrae   Space explorers land on a mysterious planet which finally proves to be none other than earth, its name often cunningly disguised by being written backwards, in an obscure dialect of Eskimo or by being called something clever like Solthri (Sol Three, get it?). This, and the Adam and Eve story, have been dubbed 'shaggy god' tales by Michael Moorcock, who read a lot of them while editing the British sf magazine, *New Worlds*.

Who was that lady I saw you with last night?   That was no lady, that was his mum, is the cry of the writer who takes his time-traveller into the past to find his missing father *only to discover that he takes on the role himself!* Gosh, thinks the writer who comes up with the notion, rubbing his hands together with glee. Yawn, thinks the reader who encounters the story or its more historically resonant variations which we mentioned in Chapter 1. Time-travel and its paradoxes have by no means been exhausted as fruitful themes in science fiction, but most of the obvious options have already been tried so that their surprise value is now zero.

Von Daniken was here   This describes a whole class of stories which employ spurious history or mythologies given a technological guise – the sort of thing popularised by Eric von Daniken in *Chariots of the Gods?* In such stories we may discover that aliens from a distant planet founded the first human civilisations, or that Atlantis was destroyed in a thermo-nuclear war, or that Stonehenge is really an amazingly sophisticated computer, built as a result of arcane wisdom which has now been lost. Anything involving arcane wisdom of whatever description is better avoided. Again it is not impossible to write good stories using notions of the kind described above; but it is very easy to descend into triteness. Similarly sf stories about unidentified flying objects tend to be predictable and rather dull; contrary to popular belief, people who are interested in science fiction are more sceptical than average about the existence in the real world of flying saucers and the little green men who are supposed to inhabit them.

Relentlessly the invaders attacked   And relentlessly our hero blasted their spaceships out of the sky. This has been a popular story in recent years, the impression being given that a real space battle is taking place until all the ships have been destroyed, whereupon the words GAME OVER suddenly appear – lo and behold, it was only a video game after all, surprise, surprise. The only surprise on the reader's part is that this already hoary old gimmick is being trotted out again.

These are just a few overworked storylines. There are many more. Stock figures include the computer which acquires godlike powers or murders its creator; the human being who turns out to be a robot or a shape-changing alien; the mad scientist who builds a death-ray in his back garden from spare radio parts; the starship engineer who repairs a ship's warp-drive with a bent paperclip. They are all clichés because we have encountered them many times before. They represent a funda-mental failure of the imagination because the writer has gone for the easy option. The best writers can, of course, breathe fresh life into the most hackneyed situation by thinking up new ways to subvert the reader's expectations; but it is a dangerous game for the new writer to play.

3
Plot and Narrative

A piece of fiction is a series of invented incidents involving invented characters. The *plot* is what actually happens — it is the action which illustrates the story's theme. For the purposes of this chapter, the *narrative* is taken to mean the actual words which constitute the story, including dialogue, characters' thoughts, and so on. It is the window through which the reader views the action.

Plot

In *Aspects of the Novel* E. M. Forster distinguishes between story and plot by saying that both are sequences of events but that plot also involves causality.* So 'The spaceship flew to Mars and Jupiter' is a story, whereas 'The spaceship flew to Mars and Jupiter because the pilot intended to explore the solar system' is a plot. Plot involves occurrences which do not arbitrarily follow on from one another; it is about cause and effect. Most science fiction is heavily plotted.

The essence of a good plot is that it should surprise the reader in some way. In science fiction, readers are always trying to anticipate the writer, and while it may not be fatal if they do guess what is going to happen, it obviously reduces the impact of the story. The very word 'plot' suggests a conspiracy, and usually it is a conspiracy on the writer's part to arrange matters in a story so that readers are kept guessing. This may be done deliberately by withholding crucial information until the last minute, or — a particular favourite with sf writers — by making readers assume that they understand the ground-rules in a particular story and hence lead them into making assumptions which are proved to be incorrect. The important thing here is that writers must *play fair* in concocting their surprises, so that if a rabbit is pulled out of a hat, then the existence of the hat should already have been implied and perhaps also the possibility that there was something inside it.

*In this book, 'story' is generally used to mean a work of fiction of any length up to and including a novel; only in this paragraph is it used in Forster's sense.

Robert Sheckley's 'The Store of the Worlds' is a short and effective tale with a neat plot twist. The story begins with the visit of a man called Mr Wayne to a small shack where another man, Tompkins, has invented a method for allowing anyone to enter temporarily the dream-world of his or her choice where their wildest desires can be satisfied. The experience takes ten years off the person's life, and so, in the story, the author tells us that Mr Wayne decides to think over whether to make this sacrifice. He does so as he walks home to his house where his wife and children are waiting for him. He considers for several weeks while working in his office and taking his wife and son sailing. As the weeks turn into months, minor domestic disasters occur, the larger world is worried about the nuclear arms build-up, but the picture is essentially of someone leading an ordinary and contented life. A whole year goes by. And then Mr Wayne wakes up — in Tompkins's shack. The entire experience has been a dream, Mr Wayne's cosy domestic bliss his ideal world. The real world has, in fact, already been devastated by nuclear war, and Mr Wayne has no family left. The story leaves him picking his way through the rubble, hoping not to miss the evening's potato rations.

'The Store of the Worlds' has a neat plot in that readers are pleasantly surprised to discover that they've been duped. Robert Sheckley constructs the story so that we slip effortlessly from the reality of Tompkins's shack into Mr Wayne's private fantasy without knowing that we have done so. At the start of the story he describes the shack as lying at the end of a long mound of grey rubble, but he says no more, so that the reader assumes he is simply describing a run-down quarter of an otherwise ordinary town or city. Only later, on discovering that the whole city has been reduced to piles of rubble, do we realise that a clue was planted and hence the author played fair. But 'The Store of the Worlds' is a good story not simply because it surprises us effectively; a genuine sense of poignancy is evoked by the discovery that the best of all worlds for Mr Wayne is the kind of world which we now take for granted. The story has a point beyond that of simply tricking the reader.

Good plots combine a sense of firm authorial control with a feeling that something unexpected could happen at any moment. Real life is often shapeless, but *fiction is a stylised representation of reality*, whether it is a kitchen-sink drama set in the here and now or a far-future space epic. A writer has a purpose in telling us a particular story, and this will be implicit in how it is organised. Plot implies structure, either hidden or overt, a sense that there is a motive on the writer's part for showing us particular things and giving us particular information. Should the structure of the story begin to stifle the characters or require a sequence of events which is too rushed or too coincidental, then it may be overplotted. Ideally the writer will have a framework within which the characters can breathe naturally and have a degree of spontaneity.

Narrative

Given that you have an idea and plot in mind, then the next step is obviously to begin writing, i.e. to produce a narrative. If narrative is the window through which the reader views the story, then it should be as transparent as possible, even if some things beyond the glass are deliberately hidden from the reader to begin with.

A major principle of good narrative is that it is better to *show not tell*, particularly as far as important incidents in a story are concerned. If you can directly describe a scene as it is happening by showing how characters speak, think and react this will make the story more vivid than if incidents are reported second-hand.

As always, however, there are plenty of exceptions to this rule. Often there are good reasons for telling rather than showing. In 'The Store of the Worlds' Mr Wayne's activities in his perfect world are reported to the reader rather than being shown first-hand, and this, as well as giving the tale conciseness, is actually in keeping with the fact (unknown to the reader at the time) that Mr Wayne is actually in a dream-like state where time is condensed. His specific activities at this point are less important than the sense of security and comfort which they suggest.

A more extreme example of a whole story being told rather than shown for good dramatic reasons is 'The Liberation of Earth' by William Tenn, which features the conflict between two advanced alien races who successively invade Earth and fight one another there, destroying much of the planet in the process and reducing the few human survivors to a borderline existence. The tale is recounted by a survivor after the aliens have finally left Earth, and it consists of a deadpan reportage of their ruinous activities and their continual assertions that they have simply come to protect the human race. The resulting tone is one of heavy sarcasm which is very effective in highlighting the hypocrisy of so-called wars of liberation which destroy the peoples they are supposed to be saving.

Where to begin?

It is usually best to begin the plot of a story as late as possible, though not at the expense of overbalancing the story with too many flashbacks or inordinate amounts of background information. Dropping the reader into the middle of a scene is often effective because it suggests a ready-made world. A particular favourite with science fiction writers is the striking opening line which immediately presents the reader with something unusual. So, for example, a story might begin:

'The man was six months pregnant, his unborn child hanging in·a transparent womb-sac at his waist.'

There are two basic responses to this sort of line. The first is to think 'That doesn't make sense. I'm not going to read any more of this nonsense.' The second is 'Now what's going on here? I must find out more.' The two responses separate the reader who is never going to have any affinity with science fiction from the reader who is going to delight in it. To one the paradox is completely off-putting; to the other it is an instant challenge.

Readers familiar with sf will immediately start inferring things from the line above. They will probably assume that the man is ordinary in all other respects apart from being pregnant. Is he a subject in an experimental programme? Or is his condition commonplace? If the latter, then this implies a society where biological science is far more advanced and perhaps the reproductive roles are equal or even reversed. Is the womb-sac detachable so that either mother or father could wear it? Do women exist at all, or have men found some means of doing away with them entirely? All sorts of possibilities present themselves.

Striking opening lines are sometimes called 'grabbers'. They can be effective in hooking the reader, but they should be used sparingly, otherwise they become a mannerism. And they should never be used if they don't lead on to a properly developed story.

Viewpoint

The viewpoint is essentially the eyes and mind through which the reader experiences the story. The three most common viewpoints in fiction are first person singular, third person singular and omniscient:

'Halt!' I ordered the robot, certain that it meant to attack me.
(First person)

'Halt!' she ordered the robot, certain that it meant to attack her.
(Third person)

'Halt!' she ordered the robot, certain that it meant to attack her, though it was actually friendly and was trying to warn her of another robot creeping up behind her, quite determined to kill.
(Omniscient)

First person may be favoured by writers because of its immediacy. The reader is more easily drawn into the story because it is often easier to identify with the 'I' character who is telling the story. Its drawbacks are that any action which does not actually involve the 'I' character cannot be shown directly, and the reader knows in advance that the 'I' character will survive whatever adventures lie in store. (Any first-person viewpoint story which ends 'And then I died' is definitely a no-no – unless, of course, the story continues into an after-life, which admittedly is perfectly possible with a science fiction story.)

Third person is the viewpoint most commonly found in stories, chiefly because it allows writers more flexibility. This may not be obvious at first, a third-person viewpoint seeming to offer all the disadvantages of the first person and few of the advantages. But third-person narratives are often split between different characters in the story, allowing the writer more flexibility. Third- and first-person viewpoints may also be combined.

Where stories are told from more than one viewpoint, the change from one to another should usually be clearly signalled in the text, perhaps by leaving a line-space. Readers tend to 'live' a given scene through the character first established as their eyes and mind, and writers need to have very good reasons for switching viewpoints in the middle of a passage. Usually it is a practice better avoided because it may disorientate the reader and suggest sloppiness on the writer's part. (Here again, however, the best writers can break the rules effectively. In 'Fondly Fahrenheit' Alfred Bester writes about an android with a split personality, giving us a deliberately muddled viewpoint which also provides the striking opening line: 'He doesn't know which of us I am these days, but they know one truth.')

Omniscient viewpoints are effectively those of the author, a god-like presence who may reveal anything and everything about the story and even comment on it as it progresses. (In the example given above, we are told the motives of all three characters.) This may have its attractions, but it is a freedom that is easy for the writer to abuse. Dramatic tension may be defused because readers are told too much, or alternatively they may feel cheated if information is deliberately withheld at a crucial point. Or the all-knowingness of the author's voice may simply be irritating. Omniscient viewpoints tend to be best suited to stories in a humorous or satirical vein, imposing a certain distance or formality on events that might seem too absurd if told through the eyes and minds of direct participants in the action.

Narrative drive

Narrative drive is a measure of how effortlessly the reader is carried through a story. It doesn't mean that the story should proceed at breakneck speed or that the reader must constantly be pitched into scenes of high drama. Essentially it involves the most economical use of words in keeping with the demands of the story.

Here are two versions of the same passage:

> The starship loomed like a black shadow on the runway. The runway was a white ribbon, and the man advanced down it, his pistol in his hand. He saw that the main hatch of the starship was open. He hesitated, then climbed through it. A corridor stretched ahead of him. He walked along it and came to a door at the end. The door opened like a pair of metal eyelids. The room beyond was in darkness, and all was silent. Then suddenly the room blazed with light. In front of him was a woman with tentacles writhing on her head. Before he could move, she came scuttling towards him, one of the tentacles whipping the pistol from his hand.

> The starship loomed like a black shadow on the white ribbon of the runway. Pistol in hand, the man advanced towards the open main hatch. He hesitated, then climbed through it. A corridor stretched ahead of him. At its end was a door which opened like a pair of metal eyelids. The room beyond was silent and dark, but suddenly it blazed with light. In front of him was a woman with tentacles writhing on her head. She came scuttling out, one of the tentacles whipping the pistol from his hand.

Now both versions are lurid, and neither aspires to any elegance or subtlety. But the second has more narrative drive than the first. It reads a little more smoothly, seems slightly less 'stiff'. The first passage has the sense of 'He did this and then this happened', suggesting that the writer's camera-eye is sedulously describing things one at a time. The second passage conveys 'As he was doing this, this happened', giving a better fusion between action and incident and allowing the writer to avoid the repetition of words such as 'door' and 'room' and to get rid of superfluous phrases such as 'He walked along it' and 'Before he could move', since these are implied in what is happening. Description is more intimately linked with action.

Texture

A typical story will contain a mixture of description, dialogue, action, reflection and exposition. These in turn will determine the *texture* of the narrative – how vividly and with how much variety the world of the story is brought alive for the reader.

Description may range from a detailed portrait of a planet's terrain to a passing mention that a character has crocodile skin. It usually adds denseness and colour to a story, rooting it in a given place or making it easier for the reader to visualise characters and what is happening to them. A particular feature of certain kinds of science fiction is that they cannot always draw on standard images to help this process of visualisation. The sentence 'He got out of his Rolls-Royce and entered the cathedral' will immediately suggest fairly specific images to most readers (or Western readers, at least), whereas 'He got out of his Q-8 floater and entered the Edifice of Sanctity' may bring no obvious picture to mind. But in fact the difference is more apparent than real. Science fiction readers will be familiar with the idea of a floater and will understand that an Edifice of Sanctity is jargon for a religious building of some sort. Of course each reader may then visualise them in quite different ways, but so, to a lesser degree, will readers encountering the Rolls-Royce and the cathedral, imagining different models and colours for the car, different styles of architecture for the building. Even so, it is often incumbent on the sf writer to make more descriptive effort in such circumstances if specific images are required.

Jargon is a shorthand form of description which may also have the useful side-effect of suggesting changes in language in the future or on other worlds. Its descriptive value often relies on familiarity, hence the fact that it need not be explained ('starship' and 'android' are two examples); or the meaning of the invented word may be obvious from its context. Typical coinages include 'conapt', used by Philip K. Dick to denote an apartment in a large building; 'waldo', used by Robert Heinlein to mean a device for amplifying the human musculature; and Ursula Le Guin's 'ansible', an instantaneous communications device. Writers may invent jargon to suit their purposes, but it should be used sparingly and generally it is better if the invented word suggests its own meaning rather than having to be explained in detail.

Dialogue will be considered more fully in the next chapter. In terms of a story's texture, it is an obvious counterbalance to all the other elements of a story, not least because it breaks up paragraphs of text. As well as helping to bring characters alive and show them interacting, it also conveys information in digestible chunks. But writers should beware the temptation to let dialogue carry the whole of the story, as descriptive colour and imaginative depth may then be sacrificed so that the story reads like a dressed-up version of a script for actors.

Action may involve anything from a space battle between fleets of starships to someone walking through a door. It is a means not only of advancing the story but also of giving it more *scope* by taking readers to different places in the fictional world and showing them its sights. Some writers may favour lots of action for the same reason that others favour lots of dialogue: it is easy to write, and it carries the reader along. In fact, though, it is hard to write well. Blow-by-blow accounts of events may result in a ponderous, schematic feel to the text, while too sketchy a passage may fail to orientate the reader properly so that what happens is muddled and difficult to visualise. Clarity and economy are the watchwords here, and these are best achieved by imagining a scene as vividly as possible before it is written. Then the essential details are more likely to be conveyed.

Reflection: reflective passages are a means of entering into the thoughts of characters. Since action, speech and thought are three major ways in which characters declare themselves in a story, reflection will always add richness as long as it doesn't consist merely of recapitulating the plot. It may also be used to add subtlety and complexity to a story, as, for example, when a character's thoughts about what is happening are later proved to be misleading or incorrect. It also helps with the pacing of a story, perhaps slowing it down after a hectic period of action, or helping to increase the tension when something is about to happen. Too much reflection will bog down a story, but too little may make it feel shallow. Prose fiction can give us characters' thoughts with a flexibility and variety unparalleled in any other narrative form, and this strength should not be neglected.

Exposition entails the conveying, for the reader's benefit, of background information necessary to fix a story in place and time. Typically in sf this means some explanation of how the world of the story came into being. The best writers will weave such information invisibly into the unfolding narrative, but this is often more than usually difficult in science fiction, which by its very nature tends to deal with invented worlds. The historical novelist who sets a story in Elizabethan England can assume that the potential readership either has a certain knowledge of the period or can verify it elsewhere. But the science fiction writer taking us into a far-future Earth or another planet can make no such assumption. Immediately there is the problem of having to explain something of how the world of the story came into being.

A particular tendency of the new writer is to settle for the 'expository lump' – a wodge of background information inserted as an undigested lump into the story. So we are happily reading along when suddenly we encounter a paragraph beginning 'Professor Prendergast had invented the photon-fractionator in the summer of 2020'. There then follow several paragraphs or pages explaining how the professor's marvellous invention led to the colonisation of other worlds, unlimited energy supplies, a cure for in-growing toenails, or whatever it is that the writer wishes. Meanwhile the plot has ground to a halt. Writers may try to be more subtle than this. I'll pass it off as dialogue, they decide. This leads to the 'As you know' syndrome, wherein one character will say something like 'You're aware, of course, that Professor Prendergast invented the photon-fractionator' and another character will reply, 'Ah yes – that was in the summer of 2020, wasn't it? They then proceed to tell one another facts which they already know for the transparent purpose of getting information across to the reader.

Ideally it is better if there is no exposition at all in a story – or rather, no *visible* exposition. Whatever information needs to be conveyed should emerge naturally from the flow of the story; if this isn't possible it should be cunningly disguised so that the reader has scarcely any sense of being force-fed facts. It is also worth bearing in mind that information deliberately withheld is often more tantalising. If this is done systematically it may simply irritate, but judicious use of such a carrot and stick will often compel the reader to keep going in order to find out exactly what is happening and why.

Vividness

Vivid writing is that which creates a strong sense of the fictional world in the reader's mind. The ability to visualise a scene well is perhaps the most important of a writer's assets in this respect, but it is not the only one. Let us return to the passage about the starship and the Medusa-woman and try to make it more vivid:

> The starship squatted like a huge tarantula on the white ribbon
> of the runway. Pistol in hand, the man advanced to the reddish
> oval of the main hatch. He hesitated, then climbed inside. A dimly
> lit corridor stretched ahead of him, silent except for the cautious
> tread of his feet on the bare metal floor. This has to be a set-up,
> he thought. At the end of the corridor a doorway blinked open
> like a pair of gilded eyelids. He almost dropped the pistol in
> surprise. The room beyond was silent and dark, but out of it came
> the stench of rotting meat – a stench so strong he could even
> taste it. There was a blaze of magnesium light. Then swishing
> sounds. A woman came scuttling out, her head a mass of writhing
> tentacles. They slapped, cold and wet, against his face, and he felt
> the pistol being wrenched from his hand.

If anything, the passage is now even more lurid, and some may prefer the merciful brevity of its predecessor. But it is, nevertheless, more vivid, and not simply because of extra adjectives and description. In the first line, for example, 'squatted like a huge tarantula' is a more specific image than 'loomed like a black shadow' (whether it is very subtle is a different matter). Similarly 'a pair of gilded eyelids' is descriptively more precise than 'a pair of metal eyelids', conveying colour as well as a metallic quality. More importantly, we are no longer simply *seeing* the scene through the eyes of the man. We have access to his thoughts, hear sounds, smell and taste the creature's miasma, feel its tentacles on the man's face. In the earlier version everything is stated rather baldly, giving the prose something of a documentary feel. The new version is still crude and cheaply sensational, but the writer is at least working harder to bring the scene alive.

Appeals to the five senses — sight, sound, touch, smell and taste — undoubtedly add vividness, and sometimes it is advised that at least three of these senses should be evoked in any given scene. But again, too studious an application of this rule, like any other rule of writing, may stifle spontaneity. If writers are fully engaged with their raw material, then vividness and a good texture should emerge naturally.

Style

Most science fiction is fairly straightforwardly told since experimental narrative styles don't always mesh well with weird settings or characters. The exceptions tend to be those stories dealing with other states of mind (see Chapter 1), in which fragmented narratives may be used, unrelated scenes or images juxtaposed, normal logic suspended or perceptions warped in order to suggest new mental horizons. See, for example, the 'condensed' novels of J. G. Ballard such as *The Atrocity Exhibition*, and *Barefoot in the Head* by Brian Aldiss.

As a rule, the stranger the actual content of the story, the more traditional is the way it is told. Similarly writers would do well to bear in mind C. S. Lewis's oft quoted comments on *Gulliver's Travels* and *Alice in Wonderland*: 'Gulliver is a commonplace little man and Alice is a commonplace little girl. To tell how odd things struck odd people is to have an oddity too much.' In other words, beware the risk of having bizarre characters undergoing equally bizarre adventures. No doubt this can be made to work, but readers need some point of familiarity through which they can enter a story; only then will they be prepared to marvel at its wonders.

Every writer's style is unique, for it concerns not only choice of vocabulary and phrasing but also the way in which the writer imagines. What is in the mind's eye will affect what words are chosen to represent it. Or, conversely, the precise selection of words will determine what pictures are created in the mind.

Style should be natural and not affected, otherwise it clouds the narrative window like mist, hindering the reader's view of a story. This doesn't mean that style should be plain to the point of invisibility, merely that it should call attention to what's happening in the story and not to itself alone. Some writers do have particularly distinctive styles which the new writer may be tempted to copy — at peril. Far better to rely on your own imagination and powers of expression.

A detailed discussion of style is not the brief of this book, but a few elementary points are worth mentioning. Variation in sentence length militates against monotony, while the judicious use of simile and metaphor can add colour to a drab passage. (But don't overdo either. There is nothing more distracting for a reader than an overly metaphorical style in which things are constantly being likened to something else.) It is advisable to have a good grasp of the rules of grammar and punctuation — especially if you intend to break them for a particular dramatic reason. Language and usage are constantly changing, it is true, but good grammar means clarity and precision of expression, while good punctuation will emphasise the natural rhythms of your prose and aid readability.

On readability

At bottom, the ultimate motive of the writer is to keep the reader turning the pages. This should always be borne in mind whether you are producing lightweight entertainments or deeply felt work of an ambitious nature. Aim for readability, even if you are simply writing the story for no one but yourself. Picture a sympathetic but critical reader who would give you an honest opinion of what you have written. Is your premise interesting? Is the story well-constructed? Vivid? Dramatic? Well written? Believable?

Readability doesn't mean packing a story with frenetic action or highly emotional confrontations. These may have their place, but the best writers are able to vary the mood and pace of a story and still keep the reader interested. In science fiction the initial appeal is often to a sense of wonder — a feeling of encountering something new or unsuspected — but this alone will not be enough. The reader's intelligence and emotions should be kept stimulated throughout the story; there should be a constant sense of movement, whether physical or psychological. The reader is offering time and attention to the story, and it is the writer's job to see that it isn't wasted.

4
Characters

Ideas for stories almost always come associated with a set of characters. The cast may range from a single person to hundreds or thousands. What is indisputable is that people are necessary. Fiction involves drama, and drama is the product of tension between character and situation. The main difference between science fiction and other kinds of literature in this respect is that sf also deals with non-human characters – aliens, robots, androids, and so on.

There is a tendency for science fiction writers to create cardboard characters – that is, characters with no personality. They may walk and talk and do things throughout a story, but all that identifies them is a name. And there has long been a debate in the field as to whether traditional characterisation is either necessary or desirable. It has been argued that, since science fiction is a literature of ideas, its main concern is with philosophical rather than psychological matters; hence its characters are close to being *archetypes* who are expressive of a single human tendency – scepticism, perhaps, or blind faith, or the voice of scientific rationalism. On this basis, any attempt to make the characters more complex would simply distract from the exposition of the central 'idea'.

Such arguments have a justification in certain kinds of stories. Earlier we mentioned William Tenn's 'The Liberation of Earth' which expressly deals with populations rather than individuals. Similarly Olaf Stapledon considers entire populations and vast perspectives of millennia in some of his books, and they convey a chilling sense of individuals being reduced to insignificance when measured against the scale of the universe. (Though here it must be said that Stapledon is a writer easier to admire than enjoy, offering as he does such a lack of basic human comforts; for all his majesty, he is more honoured in the field than actually read.)

So there are cases in which conventional characterisation is irrelevant or out of place, and science fiction does tend to attract the kind of writers who are more interested in processes than people alone, more focused on situation than character.* But all too often in sf, poor characterisation is simply a result of hastiness or neglect. Most sf stories involve conventional dramatic situations, and it is here that the paucity of characterisation gives critics of the field most ammunition. Fascinating ideas are embedded in stories which lack human depth.

Creating strong characters is hard work in all kinds of fiction, and perhaps doubly hard in sf, where the writer is also wrestling with the central novelty of the idea. But this is to see idea and character as somehow in conflict with one another. In reality, they should be complementary, the one intimately dependent on the other.

An excellent example of a solidly science-based story with convincing human characters is the novel *Blood Music* by Greg Bear. This deals with the escape of a bio-engineered virus which spreads through the population of the world, causing great changes in human mental capacities and ultimately in the human body itself. Summarised in this way, *Blood Music* might appear to be just another variation on a classic sf theme, but throughout the story the plot developments hinge firmly on the personalities of the people involved. This is evident from the start, when the virus gets out of the laboratory because an unworldly and self-obsessed researcher actually injects it into himself rather than allow the sample to be destroyed. Throughout the novel the reader has a refreshing sense of scientists behaving as real people, with all the problems and personality quirks which real people possess. The fusion between plot and character is properly achieved, and the novel works splendidly as a result.

Different characters

In science fiction it is possible to identify three kinds of character which we might label the 'talking head', the 'type', and the 'three-dimensional'.

The talking head is simply a figure who inhabits the story, speaking and acting but doing nothing whatsoever which reveals any personality. Such characters exist simply to enact the plot in the most mechanical way. Since they have no personality, talking heads are completely indistinguishable from others of their ilk.

---

*It is worth noting here that sf is by no means unique in having writers of the utmost seriousness who aren't interested in depicting personality. Franz Kafka and Jorge Luis Borges are two eminent examples, Kafka being interested in processes of depersonalisation, Borges having such a strong philosophical bent that his stories are often elaborations of ideas in their purest sense.

The type is essentially a caricature, a person who displays limited and standardised responses, whatever the situation. Types can usually be summed up by one or two adjectives – the *brave* hero, the *evil* genius, the *absent-minded* professor, the *tough but fair* space captain. Types do display character quirks, but in a predictable way. Once their essential nature has been established, they aren't capable of surprising us – or at least not convincingly. If they do something out of character, then it will jar and seem unbelievable.

The three-dimensional character displays a rounded personality and hence a range of emotions and reactions. Like real people, such characters will exhibit certain personality tendencies, but these won't easily be reducible to a pat description. They differ from real people (and this is another reminder of the essential artificiality of fiction) in that the writer can reveal far more about them. In real life, we know only ourselves with any profound depth, but the innermost thoughts and secrets of fictional characters can be laid bare. Three-dimensional characters will give the reader a sense that they live a life beyond the pages of the story. If their behaviour surprises us, then it does so constructively, deepening their personality rather than being at odds with it.

Inevitably not all characters have the same space to develop in a story, so talking heads and types may be perfectly adequate in many situations. But important characters should be as three dimensional as possible since this will make the story more realistic and enable the reader to identify more strongly with what is going on.

What reveals personality?

In Chapter 3 we mentioned that action, speech and thought are three major ways in which characters declare themselves in a story, but what are the features which define personality? Here is a shortlist:

1 Appearance
2 Lifestyle
3 Habits and mannerisms
4 Inner life
5 Interaction with others
6 Speech
7 Name

Appearance The appearance of a character takes two essential forms: *innate features*, such as facial type, height, sex and *acquired features*, such as choice of hairstyle or clothes. Both may be used to suggest character, but the former is the lazier and less realistic method. For example, a writer may describe someone as, say, 'an ape-faced man'. Now this is a pejorative epithet, suggesting stupidity and perhaps brutality. The description is concise, but it does tend to relegate the character immediately to a *type*. And it is not actually very true to life since we know that in the real world people's innate features seldom give us any clue as to their underlying character. Writers who fill their stories with jolly fat men, voluptuous barmaids, and so on, are reaching for stereotypes and presenting a cartoonish view of people because not all fat men are jolly, not all barmaids voluptuous.

Having said this, physical type *can* be fairly used as an indicator of character. Someone with crabbed features may indeed look that way because of a mean spirit which has caused him to frown and scowl all his life so that his features have *acquired* a crabbed appearance. Similarly, if a fat man in a story is *shown* spending his time happily gulping beer and munching hamburgers, then obviously he is a happy fat man. But he is happy because he likes eating, not because he is fat. The distinction might seem like a subtle one, but far from it: it is the difference between a character expressing his own personality and having one imposed on him by the author simply because of his physical type. And here again physical appearance has now become an acquired rather than innate feature: presumably the fat man would be thinner (and perhaps less jolly) if he chose to eat less.

What if we discovered that the fat man was a victim of a rare disease which makes his appetite uncontrollable and gives him a false jollity? Immediately we have quite a different perspective. Similarly the voluptuous barmaid may be decked out with bleached hair and a low-cut leopardskin dress, but if we learn that outside bar-hours she is actually a telepath who works in a school for autistic children, then her character also gains depth.

Acquired features are, in general, much more revealing. Clothes, make-up, hairdos, beards and moustaches all make some kind of statement, though it may not be an obvious one. For example, the character who dresses in drab or dark clothes will not necessarily be introverted and shy; the woman who uses garish make-up won't necessarily be gregarious. The relationship between our personalities and the way in which we adorn ourselves is complex, but it always exists and can be used fruitfully in fiction.

Lifestyle Equally important is the physical environment which people choose. What kind of life do they lead?

Obvious features here are a character's choice of job, friends, home-life and leisure activities. In terms of job, it is again easy for the slack writer to reach for the obvious sterotype – the space explorer who is fearless and bold, for example. But a space explorer may not necessarily be fearless and bold: she (yes, it's a woman) may simply be fond of travel. Or we might make her into an agoraphobic who absolutely dreads each journey but is determined to overcome her fear of open spaces. In which case, she *is* bold but certainly not fearless, a much more interesting combination.

Choice of friends and home-life may also tell us a lot about a character. A man living in a modern glass tower who throws regular parties for celebrity guests is plainly a different type from the man who lives alone in a hermetically sealed cave on the dark side of the Moon. Of course, we could decide to make them the same person, leading a double life, which opens up some interesting possibilities.

Leisure activities − sports, hobbies and the like − are also indicative of a person's appetites and inclinations. Here contrast can be useful. People often choose hobbies quite distinct from their line of work. So we might have a glamorous 3-D movie star who collects Aldebaranian wart-worms, or a devout high priest who can't resist a flutter on the rhinocerhorses. Writers should beware of contrasts which are too obvious, however: the evil genius who lovingly strokes his cat while torturing captives and unleashing doomsday weapons is a cliché well known from James Bond movies and almost everywhere else.

Habits and mannerisms   These are non-essential things which people do to make themselves more comfortable or content. Habits tend to be voluntary actions, mannerisms involuntary gestures. Habits satisfy our cravings, be they physical or mental. Routine and ritual are the watchwords here. The space traveller who crosses herself every time she boards a starship is superstitious, possibly fearful and probably devout. The robot-technician who always occupies the same seat on the hoverbus to work each morning may be highly territorial, rigid in outlook or simply unimaginative. The corpse-reviver in the cryogenic centre who always puts a fresh flower in his buttonhole every morning may be something of a dandy or feels his newly revived charges might welcome the sight of a blossom, symbol of nature's bounty.

Mannerisms are often more subtle. A nod or a shrug may reveal character, depending on how they are carried out. Much of our behaviour is instinctive, uncalculated. The man who plays with his hands may be agitated or frightened, and if his fingernails are bitten right down he is almost certainly an anxious type. A woman who constantly flicks back her hair may be vain, though if she has a hunched posture and hangs her head she may be quite the reverse and is simply keeping her fringe out of her eyes. And so on.

Habits and mannerisms should never be used too relentlessly in a story, otherwise they will seem imposed rather than natural, a forced attempt to bring a character to life.

Inner life We all have basic personality tendencies, arising from a combination of heredity and formative experiences, which colour our whole outlook on life and our responses to any situation. So too with fictional characters.

It is easy to rattle off a list of adjectives describing basic personality tendencies, optimist/pessimist, strong/weak, confident/shy, sociable/anti-social, worldly wise/naive, intelligent/stupid, talkative/taciturn, active/passive, and so on. Again the lazy writer might simply settle for saying that a character is 'cowardly' or 'selfish', but most people in the real world have personalities which aren't easily summed up by a single adjective. Thus in fiction characters will also seem more realistic and rounded if they aren't too easily pigeonholed.

For example, two interesting characters might be a sad optimist and a happy pessimist. The first may have had a tragic life through ill fortune, yet still retains a belief that things will turn out well in the end. The second might be a blithe spirit who sees life to be fundamentally futile but is determined to make the best of it.

Fiction gives us access to a person's thoughts and most private actions. So while it might be dramatically weak to tell a reader that a man is miserly, it may be perfectly satisfying to show him poring over boxes filled with pennies or trying to think of a way to avoid tipping a hotel porter. Sometimes it may be revealing to have a character act in a particular way but experience thoughts or emotions quite at odds with the behaviour. (The immortal human who extols the virtues of extended life to others while secretly longing for death embodies an interesting conflict.)

In real life, most of us change relatively little in our essential outlook once our personality has been formed, maintaining the same basic attitudes and inclinations, come what may. But this is not so true in fiction (particularly in novels) where character development is usually expected and felt to be desirable. Most general novels have as their central concern not only the delineation of character but also its transformation under the pressures of a plot.

With science fiction, such considerations aren't necessarily so central, though they are not as rare as is often supposed. In sf the transformation frequently occurs in an intellectual rather than an emotional sense – typically it might involve a sudden realisation that an assumption was unjustified, a surface appearance illusory, a connection made that leads to a completely different understanding of a situation. Science fiction tends to be focused on a character's relationship with the world at large rather than specifically with other people. Even so, a strong inner life will always make this relationship more credible.

Interaction with others Any story would be pretty static and low on drama if there were no interaction between characters. (Of course, it may offer other delights, though these would be of a purely cerebral nature.) When authors speak of 'characters coming alive' they often mean that they have written a scene in which the characters interact vividly and spark off one another. Characters will always seem more real when shown in relation to others. To return to the miserly man who hoards pennies. We might instead decide to have him answering his doorbell. A woman is standing outside with a charity collecting-box. She asks for a donation. He shakes his head angrily and tells her that he hasn't got two pennies to rub together. He adds that it would be nice if someone had a charitable collection for *him*. Then he slams the door in her face before going into his bedroom and lifting his mattress to check that his stash is still there. Not very subtle, you might say, but the exchange has also revealed that the man is a liar and a hypocrite as well as a miser.

Characters' actions may directly express their personalities or introduce a range of other possibilities. Is the calm, always reasonable character (often a robot or android in sf stories) well adjusted, or does the placid, logical exterior hide a seething mass of dangerous emotions? Does the adoring behaviour of a wife to her husband reveal her absolute loyalty to him, or is she simply lulling his suspicions before she pushes him down the kitchen's waste-o-matic chute? Or is she herself an android replica of the wife whom the man has secretly murdered? A character's actions can disguise as much as they reveal.

Speech Speech in fiction is usually called dialogue, though it is perfectly possible for characters to conduct monologues to good dramatic purpose. Mostly, though, monologues tend to be interior – in other words, thought processes rather than speech.

Interior monologues and speech are fictionally presented as simplified and clarified versions of the real thing. Just as our thoughts are often jumbled, random and multi-layered, so actual speech is often rambling, hesitant and filled with repetitions and irrelevancies. In fiction we usually present a cleaned-up version of both – though it shouldn't be so cleaned up that it is indistinguishable from the narrative style of the story.

The modern tendency is to omit quotation marks for thoughts and present them unadorned except for the use of attributive verbs ('he thought', 'she reflected', etc.) where needed. Italics can be used (these are indicated in a typed version of a story by underlining once), though are best reserved for occasions when special attention needs to be drawn to the thoughts – if, for example, they are telepathic transmissions from one mind to another.

Writers with a real gift for dialogue can often give the reader an immediate idea of a character's personality by a single line of speech. Everyone has a distinct way of talking: we have a certain voice quality, a specific tone which we adopt according to circumstances, a style of talking which arises from favoured words and phrases, and a particular accent.

Voice quality is hard to convey in fiction. It is usually necessary for the writer to state that a character has a gruff or squeaky voice, and the reader will probably need reminding of this if it is important since it won't be obvious from the dialogue alone. Tone will depend on circumstances, and this too is often hard to convey by dialogue alone. An angry speech may be peppered with exclamation marks, a hesitant one by dashes or lines of dots, but if a person is talking quietly or anxiously or intently, then again the dialogue alone will probably not suggest this and reference must be made to the character's thoughts, actions or perhaps the response of those listening to emphasise the tone.

The actual style of talking is what really reflects personality. The finicky woman will speak quite differently from her vague sister, as will the brusque man from his taciturn brother. Regional speech patterns are often distinctive, but rendering them is fraught with danger, and writers should be cautious. Beware the tendency to opt for lazy characterisation by having, say, the Texan constantly saying 'you all' and the Welshman 'indeed to goodness'. These are stereotypes, not individual idiosyncrasies. Similar dangers attend accents. The writer should be very wary about using heavily phoneticised speech to convey accent and dialect. This is extremely hard to do well, and the result is usually a risible caricature. Regional slang should also be used sparingly unless a narrow geographical focus is central to the story.

Good dialogue immediately suggests something about given characters beyond the actual information conveyed in the words, without any other clues being given. Ideally a speech could not be put into the mouth of any other character in the story – admittedly, this is a tall order, but in most cases the writer can find a variety of ways for different characters to express the same thing. For example, the question 'Did you do it?' could provoke any number of responses:

'Not me, pal/mate/squire/chum/old sport.'

'Most certainly not.'

'Honest to God I never did.'

'I ain't gonna answer in case it incriminates me.'

'I'm not going to answer on the grounds that it might incriminate me.'

'Nope.'

'Who the hell do you think you're accusing?'

And so on.

Dialogue, no matter how vivid, seldom stands alone in a story for any length of time. At regular intervals it will be necessary to identify the speaker, most commonly by adding 'she said', 'he replied', etc. Don't over-use variations of 'said' because you are worried about it appearing too many times in the story. 'Said' is what we might call an invisible word (like 'a', 'the', 'and', 'of', and so on) in that it can be used frequently without calling attention to itself. By contrast, if a story is filled with variations such as 'averred', 'stated', 'responded', 'remarked' etc., then these do become obtrusive. They are far more effective when used sparingly. Stick to 'said' if it springs naturally to mind.

In Chapter 3 we warned against having characters lecture one another so that the plot information can be conveyed in large chunks. This warning prefigures a more general point that dialogue is most effective and believable in relatively small doses. Characters who speak uninterruptedly for more than a paragraph at a time may tend to bore or distract the reader. Unless the situation specifically demands extended speech – perhaps the character is long-winded or giving a lecture – then large chunks of dialogue are best avoided because they don't parallel the way we speak in real life.

Names The importance of names in fiction is often neglected. While it would be crass to say that names should hint at a character's nature (anyone called Mordred Grim, for example, will probably be a stereotyped villain), they should not be at odds with it. In the real world it is perfectly possible for an heroic man to be called Tarquin McFarquhar, but it is much harder in fiction to prevent the reader from immediately assuming that he is a comic character. The name has a faintly ludicrous ring to it, and the writer will have to work extra hard to persuade the reader that this is a man to be taken seriously. Similarly a shy librarian called Tootsie Lovecraft will be hard to take, as would a fat man called Stark or a thin one called Rollo.

Names should be easily memorable and distinctive in some way. Mary Jones and John Smith are perfectly acceptable names, but because they are so common they may suggest an anonymity or everyday quality that the writer doesn't want. A name such as Bernard Charles could cause confusion if the character is referred to as 'Bernard' at one point and 'Charles' at another, in which case they might suggest two

Christian names and hence two separate people. A writer who to no obvious purpose has different characters in the same story called Anne, Anna and Annette, or Mulligan, Milligan and Millikan really should know better.

Made-up names – a speciality of sf – should not provoke unintentional hilarity or be unpronounceable. Thus Lorne Mowa and Count Ublezinz would have to be comic characters, while Xytptl and Wdnersphutz look like random typing. A handy technique for making up names is to consult an atlas and alter selected vowels or consonants in the names of exotic foreign cities and towns. This has to be done carefully, but it can be useful in suggesting cultural unity if all the characters in a story have names adapted from a particular geographical region.

For many writers, finding the right name is often the key to a character because it immediately sets off all sorts of resonances and possibilities. The moral of this is simple: choose names carefully. They can be a real help to the writer or a distinct hindrance to the reader.

Non-human characters

Robots, androids and aliens are familiar characters in science fiction, and they tend to be anthropomorphised – endowed with human qualities – to a greater or lesser degree.

Robots in stories have usually been built by humans, and they are often psychologically simplified versions of real people – that is, types with a single overriding personality trait. The logical emotionless robot is now so familiar that it has become a cliché, and in modern sf robots may be given other characteristics such as the fussiness of C3PO in the film *Star Wars* or the paranoia of Marvin in *The Hitchhiker's Guide to the Galaxy*. The android who perfectly resembles a human being both physically and psychologically will obviously need to have its artificial nature made known to the reader at some point in the story, otherwise it might just as well be flesh and blood. The disembodied computer program may scare us precisely because it suddenly begins behaving just like a human being.

Aliens, too, are frequently made in our image. Really bizarre alien life-forms, like Lem's sentient ocean, are more akin to supernatural forces than characters, and writers tend to prefer aliens who can actually be described as 'characters' and whose behaviour can be used to compare and contrast with our own. In appearance, too, there is often a resemblance, at least to the extent that some form of physical or vocal communication is possible. The problems of depicting a truly alien intelligence are challenging, but such an intelligence would probably cease to be a character in the conventional sense.

All the main features of human personality can be used to develop non-human characters. We might have a robot with a habit of retracting its head into its shoulders, an android with no concept of personal space who stands nose-to-nose with humans, a computer program that is bashful or tells awful jokes, an alien who smells like a hyacinth while looking like a corkscrew of smoke. The possibilities are endless.

Intelligent animals also feature in science fiction, again usually strongly anthropomorphised. Writers are wise to remember certain biological facts, however. The educated chimpanzee might be able to do algebra but it wouldn't be able to talk unless its larynx had been modified for the purpose. An intelligent cat, even if human-sized, would probably not sit upright at the dinner-table or walk about on two legs, because it is not built that way. Certain instinctive behavioural patterns would in all likelihood remain. In the real world, dolphins and whales may well be highly intelligent creatures, but we have found no effective means of communicating with them except in a simplistic way. There may be a huge gulf of understanding between different species of advanced life-forms, and the task of imagining them has scarcely begun.

Finding your characters

Happy is the writer whose characters emerge naturally from a story as three-dimensional creations. More often the writer has to struggle to bring them to life. What about basing them on people you know from real life? This practice is best avoided, especially if you intend to do it directly. There is always the danger that the real person might recognise the portrait and feel it to be unfair, inaccurate, scurrilous or whatever. (And he or she will almost certainly be right, even if the writer has honestly attempted to portray them accurately. None of us know other people so well that we can present a perfect picture of them.) Which is not to say that writers shouldn't use *traits* which they observe in others: that is both necessary and inevitable. It *is* worth studying people in the real world – looking at their dress, mannerisms, listening to how they speak, and so on. But it is best if these observations are then relegated to the compost-heap of the imagination where they will mix and mature, and eventually develop into realistic but properly fictional characters.

Failing this, the writer can make potted descriptions of various characters as an aid to bringing them alive. Here are two examples:

Alanna Henderson: woman, 33, rainbow hair, tall, good-looking, computer astrologer in Procyon City; sociable but self-centred, aggressive towards authority figures but vulnerable; fondness for luminous orchids and black cheroots; mystic tendencies underlaid by pragmatic nature; favours flowing dark clothes with lots of frills; talks rapidly in short sentences, waving her arms for emphasis.

Vérédanis: ambassador from Epsilon Eridani II, humanoid alien of indeterminate sex; vertical almond-eyes, wrinkled apple-skin face; a grimace indicates happiness, a pout puzzlement; dressed in a garment resembling ragged bandages (nicknamed 'The Mummy'); asthmatic breathing (used to high oxygen content in air); stooped posture (prefers lower gravity to Earth's); talks in a whispery voice and renders *ch-* sounds as *th-* (confusion between 'chief' and 'thief'?); slow-moving, gives off an odour resembling bitumen; can sense human emotions by a process analagous to smell.

Potted biographies of this sort can be useful, though it is wise to leave gaps so that the character can grow, or be prepared to change the details should the circumstances of the story demand it. Remember that in most cases strong characters will not merely make a plot more realistic, but they should actually motivate that plot so that they are intimately connected with what happens at every stage.

5
The Anatomy of a Story

A practical example is worth any amount of theorising, so let us follow a short story through from conception to completion. Space doesn't permit a detailed analysis of how every line came into being, but we can look at some of the most important stages.

Here is how a story I wrote recently began life:

The idea

I had been impressed by the film *Amadeus*, which portrays the rivalry between the composers Salieri and Mozart. Salieri, an established figure, recognises the natural genius of the young Mozart but despises him for the profligate life which he leads. He himself is a hard-working composer and a favourite of the king, but he knows that he doesn't have a talent to compare with Mozart's. Driven increasingly by jealousy and frustration, he finally poisons the younger man.

The idea of someone who is painfully aware of his inadequacies as an artist appealed to me, and I began to wonder about the reverse situation. What if the genius was the older man, and the lesser artist a pupil who knows that he can't hope to emulate his master's achievements? My initial idea for a story involved the apprentice waiting at the master's bedside as he lay dying, very uncomfortable in the knowledge that he will never be able to fill his shoes. But this was a rather static situation, with precious little potential for dramatising the conflict which I was anxious to explore.

So I began to consider the idea in a more science-fictional context. I needed a little novelty value, and the best place for this would be in the creative work which the characters do. What kind of artists would they be? I needed something new.

I have often thought that when readers ask writers where they get their ideas, they somehow imagine that ideas are floating around invisible in the air and can be grasped by anyone who knows the secret. What if this were literally true? What if there was a society where the very air was filled with unseen creatures like phantoms, which could be summoned into concrete existence by the mental powers of human beings sufficiently well 'attuned' to them? They could be 'condensed from thin air' into whatever shape the artist wished, given movement, colour, an appearance of life if necessary.

As a metaphor for inspiration, the idea of the creatures struck me as having the virtues of directness and simplicity. That their ultimate shape depended on the will of the artist reflected the real-life situation both specifically (as in the case of a sculptor, who is responsible for chiselling every detail out of the stone) and more generally (as with a pianist, who will bring a particular interpretation to a standard score). There was scope for plenty of concrete imagery – something that would be needed to offset any tendency for the story to dwell on abstract issues of creativity.

The plot

I had already decided that, as in *Amadeus*, the lesser talent would murder the greater, but the problem now was to find a plot which wouldn't reprise the film exactly. The story finally emerged full-blown in all its essential details when I realised that it should start immediately *after* the murder had been committed. It would involve an inquest devoted to finding out why the apprentice has killed the master, to whom he had previously been devoted. The apprentice himself would have committed suicide immediately after the murder.

The characters

This plot gave me the three main characters I needed: the master, his apprentice, and the apprentice's wife. It was she who would be summoned to the inquest, and she through whose eyes and mind the story would unfold. Other characters would obviously be needed, but they would emerge in their proper place. These three were the backbone of the story.

I made no character notes before beginning writing because I felt that I had a sufficiently clear idea of the important three. The master would obviously be a genius, supremely confident and very easy with his art. The apprentice would be a hard-working but tormented man, very conscious of his shortcomings. His wife would be in a state of shock after the two deaths, but we would see her as a practical woman who is determined to cope and who finally comes to understand why her husband killed the master.

The background

Where would the story be set? I decided not to specify this. It would be a world resembling Earth (perhaps Earth itself), with nothing too distracting about it which might dilute the impact of the art-forms. (In other words, no exotic scenery or creatures.) I felt strongly from the outset that it should have no technological trappings: this was a story about talent, about the difference between being a good artist and a great one, and I wanted very much to concentrate on the natural abilities of human beings working without artificial aids. So this would be a 'low-tech' society, the surroundings made somewhat plain so that the brilliance of the art-forms would be highlighted.

As for the art-forms themselves, no explanations would be given as to why there are unseen creatures which can be materialised, or what the creatures are. In the society of the story, it will simply be taken for granted that they exist. Many of the inhabitants will be able to sense their presence, but relatively few will be able to materialise them out of their phantom existence.

Finally, in order to remove the setting from any specific culture as we know it, I would invent completely new names for the characters — a time-honoured practice among science fiction writers. To me, finding the right names for the cast of a story is always vital, and in this case I scribbled on a pad for half an hour or so until I had a shortlist of concoctions which either sounded euphonious to my ear or simply seemed suited to the particular character that I had in mind. At last I was ready to begin writing. Here is the story that resulted.

At dawn she packed the children off to her mother's, then wandered around the empty house, checking that the doors and windows were locked. She lingered awhile in her husband's study, where the presence of the few remaining chimeras was strongest. They flittered unseen in the silence and shadows, forlornly seeking the mind that would never now make them discrete. They were like a whisper of wind, a movement not quite glimpsed from the corner of her eye; restless, abandoned. In a matter of days they would all be gone, and she would be left with memories and relics.

The house was roomy, but they had bought it as much for the large walled garden, now filled with many of her husband's earliest creations. There were some geometric and crystalline forms — exercises in abstract art — but most were figures: angels and lovers and dancers and waifs, a gallery of characters, once animate and gaily coloured, but all now ossified into grey stone.

All, that is, except for Kumash's final work, incomplete and now never to be completed. It hung in the air near the iron gate, the fleshed-in body of a faceless man grappling with the upper half of a translucent figure, as if trying to wrench it into existence. Kumash had worked almost a whole season on it but had not yet brought it to life. And now it would never be finished.

A steady rain began falling as she made her way down the hillside to the town. She tugged the hood of her red cloak down further, grateful for its enveloping warmth, grateful for the leather boots which kept out the mud. At least we are not poor, she thought. At least I can travel with a shred of dignity.

The town had grown since Vendavo had made his home there half a lifetime ago; she had been a child then. The hostels in particular had prospered, for visitors came at all seasons to see the Master's chimeras newly sprung from his brow. A small group were standing on the outskirts even as she passed by, watching a cluster of figures do a bravura aerial dance.

The chimeras' golden faces were radiant, their beauty and the grace of their movements marking them immediately as Vendavo's creations: no one else could have put such life into them. Their garments flashed in brilliant spectral hues which lit the rain-filled gloom and the rapt faces of the onlookers, who were heedless of the wetness and the wind. They looked away only at the insistence of a small boy, who wandered around the crowd, prodding them with a collecting bowl into which they happily tossed coins. One of the Master's many grandchildren, no doubt.

She hurried by before any of the crowd could notice her, turning down the muddy road towards Laaphre's spired mansion. The summons had come the previous night, a note pushed under the door and signed by Enthor, the chamberlain. Two Inquestors had arrived from the capital to pronounce judgement on her husband. They wished to interview her the following morning, in the mayor's residence.

Luck was with her, for the rain had emptied the streets; the few who passed her were huddled under their hoods. Laaphre, kindly to the last, had appended a handwritten note to the summons suggesting that she take one of the side entrances into the mansion via an alleyway. She soon saw why: a crowd had gathered at the front of the mansion. They looked restless, ill-humoured, scarcely entertained by the chimeras which gambolled and capered in the air above their heads. Even at a distance it was plain that the chimeras were inferior creations of Vendavo's disciples; one had even been fashioned to portray the Master, with his flowing white hair and the face of a devil-may-care sage. It attained only the status of parody.

Several of the artists and their agents wandered around the crowd, soliciting coins, but with little success. Across the square from the mansion was the white-domed templehouse where Vendavo had been murdered. The crowds were even larger there, but more orderly and respectful. They watched another of the Master's creations – a bird-like form of pastel colours – spiralling around the huge pyre-bowl where Vendavo himself had been cremated. A fire still burned in the bowl, five days on, and the mourning had not ceased.

The bird-chimera was one of Vendavo's older creations, but it still retained all its colour and vitality. Relatively few of his works had ossified, unlike those of lesser artists. Chimeras were sustained by the appreciation of their audience, always seeking crowds. Most migrated to the capital where they could revel in the admiration of multitudes, but Vendavo's creations flourished everywhere.

She crept down the alleyway and approached the entrance. A guard stood outside the door, raindrops hanging in a line from the brim of his hat. He recognised her immediately and nodded. The door was opened, and she went inside.

Down a wood-panelled corridor of warmth and mellow light. In the antechamber Enthor was waiting. She could see the unease in his face the instant he caught sight of her.

'They're ready for you,' he said. 'You'd better go straight in.'

He spoke briskly and would not meet her eyes. This was the same man who had once cornered her at a reception and told her how *marvellous* he thought her husband's chimeras were, how *talented* he was, what a *future* he had in store.

'Am I late?' she said. 'I set off in good time.'

'No, no. But better not to keep them waiting. They've already interviewed everyone else. Go straight in.'

He indicated the double doors. Still he would not look at her. She removed her cloak unhurriedly. Then she waited until he was forced to take it from her and hang it on the coat-stand. He hastened to open the doors for her. She walked past him without a further word.

The hall was far bigger than she had ever realised. At receptions it was always filled with tables, guests, the drone of conversation. Now it was empty and cavernous, her boots echoing on the gleaming wooden floor. At the far end the two Inquestors were seated behind a table.

Laaphre was standing beside them, and he gave her a wan smile as she approached. She felt certain that a trail of muddy footprints marked her passage. The elder of the two Inquestors was a stout woman of middle age; her companion was a younger man who blinked at her from behind wire-framed glasses. Both wore the blue tunics and the white skull-caps of their profession.

She stopped in front of the table; there was no chair for her. The Inquestors had a clutter of papers and documents in front of them, but both were scrutinising her. The woman looked severe and judgemental, the young man rather ill at ease. His lighter blue tunic marked him as an apprentice, learning his subtle trade under the woman's guidance.

'This is Caro,' Laaphre said to the Inquestors. 'Kumash's wife.'

'My name is Eshmei,' the woman told her formally. 'And this is Yanoyal. We are here to give a verdict on your husband's case.'

Your husband's case. A perfectly neutral and innocuous way of describing it. As it they were about to discuss some civil affair such as a dispute over property or the execution of a will.

'It was a terrible shock to her . . . ' Laaphre began.

'I'm sure she's perfectly capable of speaking for herself,' Eshmei said. 'I think you can leave us now.'

Reluctantly Laaphre withdrew, raising his hands to Caro as if to say that he had done what he could. When the door closed behind him, Caro felt totally exposed before the Inquestors. She decided to try to get it over with as quickly as possible.

'What do you want to know?'

'The most obvious question,' said Eshmei, 'is whether you consider that your husband was mad.'

'Mad?'

'Insane. Not in full possession of his faculties. Particularly in the period leading up to the murder. It could have an important bearing on our verdict.'

'He was not mad.'

'Consider carefully. Bring your reason to bear on the question, not your emotion. The facts in this case are as clear as they can be. All that remains is the question of motive, of *culpability*. Did your husband kill Vendavo because he was deranged, or was it a premeditated act?'

'He was not deranged.'

'Then in your view it was premeditated.'

'I'm not saying that, either. I'm simply saying that my husband was not mad.'

'If he was not mad, then it must have been premeditated.'

'That isn't for me to judge.'

Eshmei made a sceptical sound. She picked up a paper without looking at it. 'We've heard from other witnesses – Mayor Laaphre included – that Kumash had been under pressure of late.'

'He had been working long hours on a new creation, putting great effort into it.'

'So would you say he was under strain?'

'That depends on what you mean by 'strain'. Many artists experience mental pressure to a greater or lesser degree. Often it's what helps give their work vitality.'

'Let me put it more plainly. Would you say Kumash was behaving normally in the period leading up to the murder?'

'I saw little of him. He was engrossed in his work.'

'You were his wife. You lived in the same house together.' Eshmei did not bother to disguise her impatience and irritation.

'As far as I'm aware,' Caro said, 'the only strain he was under was the usual one of bringing a work to life.'

'I gather he didn't finish his latest creation?'

It was Yanoyal who had spoken, in a quiet, almost diffident voice. He peered at her indirectly, touching the bridge of his glasses.

'No,' she said. 'He didn't finish it.'

'Perhaps he despaired of creating the perfection he sought?'

'That would be more likely to make him work harder.'

'Did you love him?'

The question was unexpected, and it threw her for a moment.

'Yes,' she said. 'I did.'

'And did he love you?'

'Yes. I believe he did.'

There was a pause. Caro was expecting another question, and she saw that Eshmei was waiting, too. But Yanoyal did not follow it up.

'I am told,' Eshmei said, 'that your husband was always devoted to Vendavo.'

'That's true.'

'He was one of the Master's first acolytes, was he not?'

'He wouldn't have seen it that way. "Acolyte" implies "follower", but my husband never followed Vendavo. He was very jealous of the individuality of his work.'

'Nevertheless, he came here as a young man with the express purpose of seeking Vendavo's patronage, is this not true?'

'Yes. He recognised Vendavo as a great artist before many others did—'

'And did not Vendavo take him on as an apprentice? Did he not teach him all the necessary disciplines of his art?'

'Kumash would have been the last to deny the debt he owed Vendavo. But it was a debt of *technique*, not of *form*. Vendavo taught him the mental disciplines which enabled him to summon and materialise chimera. But the form which they took was determined only by Kumash. His imagination remained his own.'

Eshmei gave a smirk. 'Such fine artistic distinctions are doubtless of the highest importance, but alas we must concentrate on more practical matters. Your loyalty to your husband is commendable, but it doesn't seem to be getting us very far. You have two children, I gather.'

Caro nodded. 'A daughter and a son.'

'You were married soon after Kumash completed his apprenticeship.'

'Yes.'

'And Vendavo was an honoured guest at the wedding.'

'Yes.'

'They remained close friends, did they not, your husband and the Master? Until the very end?'

Kumash was still a young man when he first came here, and his father had died when he was an infant. Vendavo was more than just a mentor to him.'

'The Master's generosity was renowned,' Eshmei said. 'He was always taking in waifs and strays, isn't that true, giving anyone with the slightest talent the opportunity to learn from him?'

Caro felt a flicker of anger. But before she could say anything, Eshmei reached into one of her pockets and produced a small object which she put down on the table. It was a miniature head.

'The head was on display here at the mansion,' Eshmei said. 'Laaphre kindly let me borrow it for the purpose of this inquest. 'Do you recognise it?'

'Of course.'

'One of Vendavo's I gather. Actually, the artistry is unmistakable. It was done many years ago, wasn't it?'

The perfectly formed features of her husband's face were caught in a stony material that still retained a little of its colour, though the hair was greying and the blue eyes had faded somewhat. She remembered it as a newly created chimera, a still-life given sufficient mass by Vendavo so that it could be handled, placed on display. The Master's wedding gift to her. He had created it during the reception, almost as an afterthought. Though a minor work, his genius was stamped all over it, and lesser artists would have struggled for days to fashion something with only a fraction of its qualities.

Caro had kept the head on the mantelpiece in the living room for some years until the visiting Laaphre, in a misguided attempt at flattery, had pretended that he thought the head was a self-portrait, Kumash's own creation. Her husband's mood had been black for days afterwards. And then the head had vanished.

'I gather,' said Eshmei, 'that this object was given to Laapre as a gift by your husband.'

Caro nodded. 'He admired it.'

'Do you think your husband was jealous of Vendavo?'

'No.'

'Are you quite sure? Not the least bit jealous?'

'No. Not in the way you think.'

'And what way would that be?'

Caro felt her defences crumbling. 'Everyone knew that Vendavo was the finest artist of them all. Everyone knew he was the best.

'Your husband included?'

'Of course. Kumash continually marvelled at his abilities. But he wasn't jealous in the sense that he begrudged him them.'

'In what sense then?'

She was floundering. 'I don't know. He didn't want Vendavo's gifts. He just wanted to be better.'

'Better?'

'Better than anyone. Not just Vendavo.'

'But Vendavo was the best.'

'Kumash was devoted to him. He always acknowledged freely the help he had been given to perfect his own art.'

'It scarcely seems like an act of devotion to stab him to death inside the templehouse, in full view of several apprentices.'

The horror of it all still lived with her. She had been summoned to the temple immediately after the murder, and had arrived breathless to find that Vendavo's body had not been moved. He lay on the stone floor in front of the altar, a huddled, pathetic figure in a bloodstained white robe. His apprentices surrounded him, some weeping copiously, all staring down at his slack face, his closed eyes. Kumash was sprawled nearby, having fallen on the same knife which he had used to stab Vendavo in the heart. There was an expression of anguish on his face.

'We attach no blame to you,' Eshmei was saying. 'You must understand that. But you are an intelligent woman, and you must also understand that it is our duty to get to the bottom of this. It is important for us to establish *why* your husband committed this insane act. He has deprived the world of a great artist who still had much great art to create.

Caro could not dispute this. Old though he was, Vendavo had been in vigorous health and still at the height of his powers.

'You're asking me to pass judgement on my husband,' she said. 'I can't do that.'

'If he was not insane, then it was murder, plain and simple.'

'Yes, it was murder, I won't deny it. What more do you want from me?'

'Why did he do it?'

Caro hesitated. 'I can't give you an answer to that.'

'Can't or won't?'

'Kumash was a quiet man. He rarely spoke of his inner feelings, even to me. I was as shocked by the news of the murder as anyone else.'

Eshmei waited for more. When Caro said nothing further, she sighed, then glanced at Yanoyal. 'Is there anything else you wish to ask?'

Throughout the interrogation Caro had been aware of Yanoyal scribbling down her answers and gazing askance at her. He looked nervous, and yet he had not missed a single thing she had said.

'If I may,' he replied. He studied the papers in front of him, then said, 'You've already told us that your husband considered Vendavo to be the best artist of all. Did he have a high regard for his own work?'

'He was a perfectionist,' Caro said. 'He would never accept second best.'

'I see. In the early days of your marriage, he earned little from his art and I gather that you supported the family.'

'Yes.'

'As a washer-woman.'

'Yes.'

'Did you always support his aims as an artist?'

'Always.'

'Because you loved him.'

'Yes.'

'Was he a happy man?'

Yanoyal was still taking notes. Caro wished that he would look up from the paper. It was as if he was trying to hide his face from her.

'He set the highest standards for himself,' she said. 'That rarely leads to contentment.'

'But later his work became a critical and commercial success. Didn't this make him happy?'

'It helped ease certain pressures, but it wasn't everything. Kumash was his own sternest critic. He was never completely satisfied with what he produced.'

'He wanted to be a great artist.'

'I suppose he did. He was an orphan, and he always said that becoming an artist had given meaning to his life. He wanted to leave behind something lasting.'

Only now did Yanoyal look up. 'Thank you,' he said softly.

Eshmei was frowning, as if she deemed Yanoyal's line of questioning somewhat irrelevant. She paused for a moment, then drew herself up in her chair. 'In the light of what you've told us, I can only conclude that this was a premeditated act of murder on your husband's behalf, provoked by jealousy. The fact that he killed himself immediately afterwards may suggest that his mind was unbalanced, but I'm inclined to take the view that it was voluntary suicide. Would you have any reason to dispute these verdicts?'

'No. None.'

'Then I see no reason why we should delay you further.'

Caro went directly home, keeping to the sidestreets. No one recognised her or hindered her passage. She had imagined a long ordeal with the Inquestors, but it was all over so quickly she felt only relief. Perhaps now she could begin to plan for the future without Kumash.

The rain had stopped and the skies were beginning to clear as she climbed the path to her house. Entering the garden, she saw the havoc that had been wrought in the short time of her absence. Kumash's chimeras had been overturned and smashed to pieces, broken limbs and heads stamped into the mud, rhombs and star crystals reduced to shards scattered everywhere. Only the unfinished work above the gate was untouched, as if its incompleteness disqualified it from attack. The garden had been reduced to a morass by the tread of many feet – a mob, no doubt, who had perhaps fled on seeing her climb the path from the town.

She hurried into the house, but nothing had been disturbed there. The larder was still stocked with food, and the chest holding their valuables had not been touched. At least they're not blaming me, she thought. And then, ashamed of it, she went back out into the garden to salvage what she could.

She was righting an angel which had miraculously survived the attack when a voice came from over the wall: 'Caro? What's happened?'

It was Iriyana. Caro had not seen her since the cremation. She hurried into the garden, her orange cloak dragging in the mud.

'They came while I was at the inquest,' Caro told her. 'Smashed everything they could.'

Iriyana did not bother with words of sympathy; she simply helped Caro to search through the mud for complete pieces and fragments that could possibly be reassembled.

'It must be hard for you to forgive him,' Caro said. 'Two of your most popular clients gone at a stroke . . . '

'You mustn't blame yourself for what Kumash did. Vendavo had a long and prolific career. His works will be earning money for many years to come, and they'll live on long after we're gone. I doubt that Kumash could help himself.'

Caro began to cry. Iriyana put an arm around her shoulder until she had stopped. Then they resumed their rooting through the mud.

'How did it go?' Iriyana asked. 'The inquest?'

'I think the verdict's going to be premeditated murder.'

'And the motive?'

'They seemed convinced that it was jealousy.'

'Ah. So they've taken the line of least resistance.'

'What did you say when they interviewed you?'

'I gave them the facts as I knew them. Nothing more.'

'Perhaps I should have told them everything. You know why he did it, don't you?'

'I have a strong suspicion.'

'It was because . . . '

'No, Caro. I'd rather not be certain. It makes no difference now, does it?'

They continued tidying the garden until their arms were muddied to the elbows. The rescued remains made a pitiful sight, but Caro was sure that several of the chimeras could be repaired. And at least the garden no longer looked a shambles.

Inside the house they washed themselves with flannels and hot water.

'I'll warm some soup,' Caro said.

'Not for me,' Iriyana replied. 'I must be getting home. There's a lot to be done.'

'Thank you for helping.'

'It was the least I could do. We mustn't let what's happened come between our friendship, Caro.'

They went down to the gate together.

'I'll call in again tomorrow,' Iriyana said. She paused to stare at the faceless man wrestling with the phantom. 'You were lucky they left that one alone. I think it may well be Kumash's best work.'

'He was always so diligent once he started something. I still don't understand why he didn't finish it.'

Iriyana looked at her. 'You surprise me, Caro. I thought it *was* finished.'

Caro watched from the gate until Iriyana disappeared over the brow of the hill. Then another figure appeared. He was dressed in dark blue, and his spectacle lenses suddenly flashed gold in the sunlight.

Caro put her hands around the spears of the gate. Like a soldier behind a fortress, preparing for an attack.

Yanoyal greeted her with a nod. He was not wearing his skullcap, and his hair was cropped to a blue stubble.

'I hope you don't mind me coming,' he said, gazing at the unfinished work. 'Is this what Kumash was working on?'

'Yes.'

'Remarkable,' he said, making the word sound drab.

'What do you want?'

He adjusted his glasses. 'Eshmei and I will be returning to the capital tonight. Before we leave, there were just one or two minor points that I wanted to clear up – a few details which still perplex me. I must confess that it's the question of motive which troubles me most. Eshmei has taken the view that it was simple jealousy, yet somehow I find that rather difficult to accept. As I believe you do.'

Caro remained silent, making no move to invite him through the gate.

'I'm not here in my official capacity, of course, but merely as an interested individual. Now that the judgement has been given, nothing can alter it – short of the deceased coming back to life.' A brittle laugh. 'I simply want to satisfy my own curiosity.'

He kept his eyes on the chimera, giving her only an occasional shy glance. But his shyness was deceptive, a means of disarming suspicion. The truly diffident would never have been chosen as Inquestors in the first place.

'What do you want?' she said again.

'All the evidence regarding your husband's relationship with Vendavo indicates that he loved him and freely acknowledged his genius. But at the same time the plain fact of the murder indicates a – how shall I say it? – a *desperate* measure on Kumash's part. Something that went beyond love for any single human being.'

Still she was silent. Iron grey clouds had covered up the sun, and rain began to fall again.

'Your husband's work is very well known in the capital,' Yanoyal said. 'It's not as popular as Vendavo's, of course. But then Kumash did not quite have his genius, did he?'

Silence. Yanoyal was managing to look directly at her now, all pretence of shyness gone.

'Did your husband regret this?'

'Regret what?'

'That he did not have Vendavo's genius.'

'I answered your questions this morning. I have nothing more to say.'

'Then let me tell you what I think. I think your husband was aware of his limitations as an artist to a painful degree. A *desperate* degree. And his desperation grew and grew until he could no longer bear the idea that his work wasn't good enough. He knew he could never hope for a place in history like his master – unless. Unless he did something to ensure that his work would never be forgotten.'

The rain was beating down hard now, but she was determined not to let him into the garden.

'Do you know that your husband's creations are now more sought after in the capital than ever before? They have acquired a notoriety value – something I believe your husband specifically intended when he murdered Vendavo. If a person knows that he lacks the talent for true fame, then infamy may seem the next best option. Your husband became sufficiently unhinged with the knowledge of his limitations to see this as the only apotheosis he could hope for. His motive was not jealousy but the fanatical desire to immortalise his work.'

Yanoyal looked eager for Caro to confirm his theory. The rain lashed down, beading his glasses and soaking them both. Caro wanted to slap his face, but instead she smiled.

'I can see that you'll have no difficulty becoming a master of *your* craft. Yes, that was why he did it.'

A smile formed on Yanoyal's bloodless lips. Caro turned and walked away, entering the house and closing the door firmly behind her.

She watched him head back through the rain towards the town until he disappeared from sight. At least he would leave her alone now. She had satisfied him with a lie, and that was her consolation.

She banked the fire up, put the bowl of soup on to warm, then changed into dry clothes. Her mother had promised the children an outing to the underground lake, and she would return with them at dusk. They were taking it well, neither of them having really absorbed the fact that they would never see their father alive again. Like Vendavo, Kumash had undergone a form of cremation: he had been thrown on to a bonfire by a mob, his chimeras shunned so that they had disappeared from the town.

Memories of Kumash began to gather as she forced herself to swallow some soup. Their first meeting, both of them young, he newly arrived in the town to seek Vendavo's patronage. Their courtship, a time when he had been as passionate towards her as he always was towards his art. Visits to Vendavo's house, a place crowded with works of art and thick with unseen chimeras awaiting the Master's summons. Vendavo himself, a big, hearty, generous man, almost irreverent about his art, conjuring up brilliant chimeras while eating or drinking with his gaggle of grandchildren running around his heels and perched on his knees.

The contrast with Kumash's painstaking efforts could not have been more stark. Diligently her husband had accompanied Vendavo to the temple-house every morning, there to perfect the powers of concentration which would attract the chimeras and condense them from thin air. Kumash had never found it easy, no matter how studiously he practised, no matter how much encouragement the ever magnanimous Vendavo had heaped upon him. 'You're the best of my pupils,' the Master would tell him. 'The very best.' But that had never been enough. Her husband's tragedy was that he had been a perfectionist to whom even excellence had never been possible.

Mostly he worked behind the locked door of his study, brooking no interruptions. But she had watched him at work in the garden on his last creation. He had laboured all afternoon to bring forth the faceless figure. Sitting cross-legged on the grass, eyes closed, he had concentrated and concentrated until finally a flickering in the air had heralded the slow manifestation. At length the chimera had materialised − a ghostly figure, half in limbo, half in the visible world. Night had fallen before the shape had stabilised and acquired a feeble blush of colour.

And that was only the start. Kumash had laboured almost a whole season on the figure, shaping and refining, agonising over its every flaw. He slept badly, woke before dawn, worked every available hour on the creation. His art had never come easily to him: indeed, it became harder the more he struggled and failed to find that spark of genius.

Caro was always the first to be allowed to see his finished work. This was the moment she dreaded most of all. Kumash would be excited and anxious all at once, eager for her opinion, eager for her praise, but at the same time insistent that she be brutally frank with him. He seized on the slightest hint of prevarication, was suspicious of unqualified praise, thrown into gloom by any criticism, however minor. Whatever she said, it always ended badly.

No artist had ever worked harder than her husband, she was sure of that. None had shown such devotion, none had been more serious, none had strived harder for greatness. And success had come, financial reward and critical praise. But it was never enough, and Kumash remained acutely dissatisfied with his achievements. 'It's very good,' she would tell him, surveying his latest creation. 'One of your best.' To which he would reply: '"Good" isn't good enough! It should captivate you, transport you, take you beyond analysis or criticism. That's what all the finest works achieve. You condemn it with the very earnestness of your praise!'

She had no answer to such tirades, for there was no answering the truth. Kumash's creations were always shapely, colourful, their movements pleasing to the eye. He deserved his popularity. But he was always aware, more powerfully than anyone else, that his creations lacked the magnificence of great art.

If only he could have accepted second best. But this had never been in his nature. And so his bitterness and despair had grown, deepening with each creation. He would tell her of the brilliant visions which he held in his mind, and of how the actual manifestations failed him. Meanwhile she tended the house and raised the children. He had always been a considerate husband in his way, kind to all of them, often loving. But he had poured so much of himself into his art until finally he was drained dry.

And so deep despair had driven him to kill the very man whose greatness he could not emulate. She had known that something drastic was going to happen but been helpless in the face of it, unable to anticipate what. Only now did she fully understand why he had done it.

Yanoyal, clever Yanoyal, had been very close to understanding why. The difference between the truth and her lie was a small one, but crucial. Kumash had killed Vendavo not in the hope of immortalising his own art: he had no illusions about its lasting value. He had done it to immortalise himself. If he could not find a place in history through his own creations, then he would do so by killing someone greater than himself, become known for ever as the Master's murderer. Infamy was itself a sort of fame.

The rain had cleared, washing the landscape clean. Kumash's final creation shone in the sunlight at the bottom of the garden. She saw now that it had indeed been finished, that the faceless figure struggling with the half-formed chimera was not trying to wrench it into existence. On the contrary. The hands – they were Kumash's hands – were pushing, not tugging, intent on forcing the creature back into the oblivion from which it had come.

Afterwards

I had problems finding a suitable title for this story, and in the end I settled, rather unhappily, for 'A Work of Art'. Some readers may view the story as fantasy rather than science fiction, given that it contains no technology whatsoever and never explains what the creatures are and how human beings are able to transform the unseen chimeras into visible and material objects. But, to me, it qualifies as sf since I made some attempt to rationalise the process. The creatures aren't summoned as if by magic; they are receptive to minds which have been trained (and have the talent) to draw them out of limbo by concerted mental effort. As an idea, it is not so very different from that of telepathy or telekinesis, standard sf notions.

I began writing the story with only the bare bones of the plot in mind, so the process was chiefly a question of fleshing-out characters and situations, and developing the theme. The text given above is actually a slightly revised version of my initial draft. The revisions involved either tidying up the actual prose or clarifying details and eliminating irrelevant material. For example, at first I had three separate names for the chimeras according to the stages through which they passed: they were called 'wraiths' in their disembodied form, 'chimeras' as living works of art, and finally 'artefacts' when they turned to stone. but this was far too confusing, so I settled for using 'chimeras' to apply to all three forms. ('Chimera' seemed an appropriate piece of jargon, sounding suitably exotic and having the twin meanings 'a fabulous monster' and 'a grotesque product of the imagination'.) I also eliminated a reference to Iriyana as being an artist herself as well as an agent, specialising in doing portraits of famous criminals. I had originally intended to tie this fact in with Kumash's killing of Vendavo. But it didn't work, so I got rid of it.

I was reasonably happy with some aspects of the story as it finally emerged, less sure about others. Among the things I liked were: the chimeras themselves; the notion that older works of art decayed into stone, which gave me the idea of having Kumash's garden resemble a cemetery; the character of Laaphre the mayor, even though he is a peripheral figure; Yanoyal's apprenticeship with Eshmei, which echoes Kumash's with Vendavo; the little stone head; and the image of Kumash's final chimera.

I was rather worried about the fact that the two main characters are dead when the story opens so that we only learn about them through others. But this limitation was built into the plot and there wasn't much I could do about it except to try to make Kumash and Vendavo as vivid as possible through Caro's reflections. The plot itself relies heavily on psychological drama rather than action in the obvious sense, and I wondered if readers would find it too slow and too preoccupied with abstract issues of art rather than the chimeras themselves, which are the central novelty. But the idea of 'mind-art' is scarcely a new one in science fiction, and I wanted to remain true to my original intention of examining the relationship between an artistic genius and his less talented pupil.

So, overall I was aware that the draft of the story presented above was probably far from perfect when I took it to a writers' group (see Chapter 6), where the story was read and criticised in detail by others.

The general response was favourable, but it soon became obvious that the story needed more work. Here is a list of the main flaws which were found, with some suggestions for improvement:

1   There was some initial confusion about the relationship between Kumash and Vendavo, largely because Vendavo's name is introduced with no explanation of who he is. Are they both artists? The same person? Who did what to whom? Is Kumash also dead? This wasn't clear at first. Caro herself isn't named immediately, for no obvious reason.

2   Almost everyone felt that Caro showed an absence of feelings through most of the story which was unrealistic and tended to rob the story of emotional content.

3   The actual inquest was felt to lack bite and drama. The Inquestors' interrogation was too naive and far too gentle. They should have been more angry with her, more determined to get at the truth. And when Kumash is found guilty of premeditated murder, there should be consequences – his property confiscated, for example. The dialogue in the inquest section was also felt to be rather bare, making the passage read like a screenplay, and the verdict is given too quickly.

4   Why did the mob wait so long to vandalise the garden? It is rather too convenient dramatically. Surely a guard would have

been placed on Caro's house after the murder, and perhaps Caro would have had an escort to the inquest.

5 Most people disliked the idea of artists having agents, and not everyone realised that Iriyana was Vendavo and Kumash's agent. Caro's reference to her 'clients' was rather ambiguous.

6 No one was happy with the ending. The distinction between Yanoyal and Caro's versions of Kumash's motive was seen as tenuous and lacking in dramatic power. Another reason should be found for Kumash's murder of Vendavo.

7 Related to this, the final image of Kumash's chimera was confusing. As a symbol, it doesn't connect with Caro's theory about her husband. Caro's attitudes are also muddled. She implies to Iriyana that she knows why her husband killed Vendavo, yet she is surprised when Iriyana points out that the chimera is unfinished – a revelation which leads her to reflect that 'only now did she fully understand why he had done it'. This is contradictory.

Various other criticisms were made. For example, Caro's memories of Kumash were felt to come too late in the story, while Yanoyal's reappearance at the end was seen as another dramatic convenience. More minor points were sometimes the subject of disagreement, some people arguing that such-and-such should be altered or deleted, others insisting that it should remain.

This sort of disagreement is common when any given story is analysed by more than one person. In the end, all criticism has to be weighed against the writer's honest reactions to it. Where it is relevant it often confirms a feeling of doubt that the writer has already had, either consciously or unconsciously. If it seems misguided or arbitrary, then it is probably better ignored. Just as a complete resistance to doing any revision is usually unwise, so is the opposite extreme of making changes in response to every last quibble. Ultimately the writer is always the best judge of how a story should be reworked because no one else has a closer relationship with it. And no single work can hope to please everyone in all its details.

The criticisms I've mentioned above are the ones that struck me as most pertinent, though not all are equally serious. To me, the biggest flaw was that the ending didn't work, which meant that the story didn't effectively deliver what it promised. So I went away and thought over all the points that had been made. And then I sat down to rewrite the story.

6
Rewriting

It is a common axiom that good stories are rewritten rather than written. Unless you meticulously plan a story before writing it – and this involves anticipating all the twists and turns of plot and characters – then it is likely that the first draft will be rough-edged, containing material that is poorly organised, underdeveloped or redundant.

Rewriting is largely a question of seeing the wood for the trees. A common problem with new writers is impatience. They get an idea, and immediately they start writing. Sentence follows sentence, paragraph follows paragraph, until the story is finished. But by adopting this 'head-down' approach, the sense of the story as a whole is often lost. In the process of being written, the story may have developed a different internal dynamic which sits uneasily in the framework originally conceived for it.

The skill which most often separates the experienced writer from the beginner is the ability to produce a first draft of a story which has a good structure and thematic unity. It is a skill best developed by practice, by writing stories which 'go wrong' and have to be rescued by reworking them, sometimes drastically. In this way, the writer is forced to come to grips with the principles of good composition and good drama. Experienced writers can often 'patch up' a story simply by adding bits and deleting others rather than doing extensive revision, but this isn't a practice to be recommended to the new writer, unless the story works well from the outset. Usually it is far better to revise it thoroughly from start to finish after having examined the first draft as critically as possible.

Pinpointing flaws

Sometimes a story's flaws are immediately obvious, but not always. Often the writer is the last person to recognise the most glaring faults, particularly when it is just hot off the typewriter.

Ideally the best way of discovering whether a story works or not is to show it to someone else who will give you a fair and detailed critique. But who should you ask? Professional editors at magazines or publishing houses may seem the obvious choice, but they almost never have the time or the inclination to comment at length on fiction submitted to them (unless, that is, they are already committed to buying it). Finding friends whose opinions you can trust may be useful, providing that you *can* trust them to respond honestly and that they have an aptitude for reading stories critically. Even then, it is important to measure their responses against your own instincts.

Another (and in many ways better) approach is simply to put the story aside for a few weeks or even months. This may seem like a terrible indulgence to the writer who is eager to break into print, but the time can be used working on other stories. When finally you go back and re-read what you have written, you will be in a better position to see it with a fresh eye and as a whole unit. You will see what you have actually written rather than what you thought you had. Any flaws will be more obvious.

Every story creates its own problems for the writer – problems which demand differing solutions. It is therefore hard to be specific about what kind of revisions should be undertaken. But rewriting takes two essential forms: improving the story's *style*, and improving its *structure*.

Style

The actual prose used to tell the story should flow smoothly. Anything which is clumsy, slack or muddled should be eliminated. Awkward phrasing, the repetition of words, and passages which confuse rather than illuminate are all things which are more easily spotted if the story has been set aside for a while.

Similarly any flowery writing which may have pleased the author at the time will often appear excessive on re-reading. 'Murder your darlings' is the advice frequently given to new writers, meaning that they should ruthlessly delete any passages of which they are especially proud. This is rather dogmatic – if you are still proud of a passage some weeks after writing it, then by all means keep it – but writers are well advised to beware falling in love with their own powers of expression.

For example, a sentence such as 'The twin suns were setting below the bruised crepuscular horizon like a pair of drowsy bloodshot eyes' might seem impressive to the writer who commits it to print. But readers won't have such a rosy-eyed view: they will know it to be prose of the purest purple. Why exactly? Well, apart from being overburdened with adjectives, the word 'crepuscular' (meaning 'pertaining to twilight') suggests a rather ostentatious display of the writer's vocabulary. It is also redundant because we already know that it must be dusk, having been told that the suns are setting. The writer is too obviously striving for effect while not providing a particularly clear visual image for the reader. The needs of the story have been sacrificed to an intrusive sense of the writer's presence.

Always bear in mind that the actual words of the narrative are the window through which the reader views the story. As we remarked in Chapter 3, this isn't to imply that prose should invariably be plain or simple, merely that it should clarify rather than confuse. Anything that seems like excessive verbiage, from single adjectives to whole paragraphs, should be struck out. The story will be leaner and fitter as a result.

Related to the subject of style is the problem of conveying accurately through prose the fruits of the imagination. Sometimes words and phrases do not mean exactly what we intend them to mean. For example, the sentence: 'The man shot the alien with the ray-gun' seems quite straightforward and is grammatical enough. But its meaning is ambiguous. That the man shot the alien is in no doubt, but who is carrying the ray-gun? The man? The alien? Both?

Of course the meaning is often obvious from the context, but not always. To the writer it may be crystal-clear, but to the reader it is confusing. Again this is the sort of problem most easily solved by putting the text aside for a while, then reading it afresh – a situation which more closely corresponds with that of the innocent reader.

Structure

Structural revisions often involve much more work, and frequently they entail re-entering the story imaginatively rather than simply doing some fine-tuning. Earlier we schematically divided a story into opening, development, climax and resolution. We have also considered its creative ingredients: idea, plot, narrative and characters. From all these elements we can draw up a shortlist of basic questions which can always be usefully asked of an sf story:

1 Is the initial situation intriguing?
2 Is the story well constructed?
3 Are the characters sufficiently developed for the story?
4 Does the story deliver what it promises?

These are basically structural questions. (A fifth – 'Is it well written?' – has been addressed under 'Style', above.)

Is the initial situation intriguing? The reader must be sufficiently 'hooked' within the first few pages in order to want to read on. Some sense of conflict or mystery should be established as soon as possible. With science fiction, there is always an element of strangeness lurking somewhere, and this is what the reader will be looking for. (An associated question, especially pertinent to sf, is 'Is the reader properly orientated at the start?' It is very easy for the writer to get carried away with the thrill and wonder of the sf idea. Whatever strangeness exists in the story should be anchored to something recognisable so that the reader has points of reference against which it can be judged. Writers who use a mass of sf jargon or throw the reader into a situation where a welter of unfamiliar things are happening do so at their peril.)

Is the story well constructed? Sometimes it is relatively easy for the sf writer to think up a striking opening or a dramatic finale. But in between the story should have a continuing sense of development, with every scene and passage contributing in some way to the unfolding drama so that the reader is always kept eager to discover what is going to happen next. Anything which doesn't advance the plot or usefully inform should be cut.

Are the characters sufficiently developed for the story? Bizarre ideas and exotic settings are fine, but a convincing human dimension to the story is usually needed. The characters should be facing some dilemma, great or small, and their response to this should be coloured by their personalities. Plot and character should continually influence one another.

Does the story deliver what it promises? Ultimately this is the most important question of all. A reader drawn into any story soon develops a set of expectations. These may change during reading, but eventually they should either be satisfied or deliberately thwarted in a fair and entertaining way. Ideally, a story will express its theme as concisely and dramatically as possible.

Shaping and pacing

Finding the right shape for a story is essential. The plot should illustrate the idea or the theme with maximum reader impact. It is better if the writer has some idea of the overall shape of the story *before* beginning writing, otherwise it might go so badly awry that it has to be junked and a whole new story found.

Pacing fundamentally means organising the narrative so that the reader's sense of expectancy is kept at a high pitch. Often giving a story a better pace involves the cutting of superfluous material. If it seems 'slow' or 'bogged down' at a particular point, then it is usually because nothing essential to the story is happening; words are being used to no particular purpose.

Pacing can be aided by looking for natural breaks in the story, and the writer should never be afraid of leaving a blank line instead of writing a boring linking paragraph. For example, assume a character has to make a spaceflight from Planet A to Planet B for plot reasons. If the writer knows that nothing significant is going to happen during the journey, then it is often far better to end the scene on Planet A, then leave a space or start a new chapter which begins with the character already arrived on Planet B. Fiction, as well as being a stylised version of reality, is also an edited version of it.

A line-space is often sufficient to indicate breaks in scenes occurring soon after one another, or perhaps the transition to a different viewpoint or a different set of characters entirely. Chapters are more often used in longer stories and novels, while sections or parts may apply to bigger breaks in time or space, though not invariably. Line-spaces, chapters and sections are simply ways for the writer to organise the story for the benefit of the reader. Used intelligently, they can eliminate the need for much unnecessary writing.

Loose ends

Reshaping a story involves changing its individual parts so that they contribute better to the whole. Loose ends are story threads which don't tie up with anything else (they may be characters, incidents or scenes which aren't strictly necessary to the story). In most cases, they are better eliminated. As a painting exists within a frame, so a story should inhabit its own microcosm with a reasonable degree of neatness.

While revising the first draft of the sample story, I got rid of all references to Iriyana doing portraits of famous criminals because it distracted from the main theme rather than enhancing it. I also eliminated a detailed description of Laaphre's mansion because it was irrelevant.

Foreshadowing

This is the opposite of getting rid of loose ends. Foreshadowing entails introducing incidents or images which may have no obvious relevance at first but are later seen to be highly significant. New writers often ignore the necessity for this, especially when they are writing science fiction. They are so eager to startle that they spring revelations out of the blue. But unless subtly primed (and subtlety is important here), the reader will simply feel cheated rather than pleasantly surprised.

Proper foreshadowing is a way of ensuring that the story delivers what it promises. It also helps heighten the sense of drama. In the sample story, the description of Kumash's final chimera is given at the beginning, and the experienced reader will (whether consciously or unconsciously) 'file away' the image for future reference, having assumed that it must have some significance since specific attention was drawn to it. If there had been no further reference, then the image would have qualified as a loose end. In fact, it does recur and is made to seem central to Caro's understanding of why her husband murdered Vendavo. (But exactly how isn't clear in the story as it stands, which is why the ending disappoints.)

Let us re-examine the story and see what sort of structural revisions I might usefully undertake. Returning to the four questions asked above:

Is the initial situation intriguing? I would hope so. The opening pages are quite leisurely, but the chimeras are mentioned in the second sentence so that the reader's curiosity should quickly be aroused. What are these strange unseen creatures? What exactly are the objects in the garden? What has happened to her husband? The reader should also be reasonably well orientated, the only unfamiliar elements being the chimeras themselves and the Inquestors, whose function can be broadly deduced from their name.

Is the story well constructed? No one had any major complaints about the overall structure, or with the fairly sedate pace – though the latter will be unlikely to appeal to the action-adventure reader. The drama is psychological rather than physical, and the trial scene is weak because sufficiently probing questions aren't asked.

Are the characters sufficiently developed for the story? No. Caro in particular seems too empty of feeling given her circumstances, and we need to know more about her feelings towards both Kumash and Vendavo, preferably earlier in the story as well.

Does the story deliver what it promises? Plainly it doesn't, for reasons given above. The final revelation lacks impact and fails to tie in with the meaning of Kumash's final chimera.

Writing any work of fiction is a process of balancing blind instincts with conscious control, of letting scenes and situations spring naturally to mind, then fitting them into a satisfying dramatic framework that does not cramp or stultify them. In this case, the image of Kumash's final chimera came to me unbidden: I wasn't really sure what it meant at the time, but it was too vivid and somehow too 'right' to be ignored. It was only much later, after the story had been dissected by others, that I realised it held the key to finding the right ending to the story. I had got the ending wrong because I had imposed my own rationale on the story rather than working with the image I had been given. Caro interprets the symbolism of the chimera correctly, but she doesn't connect it accurately with Kumash's state of mind.

Revising the story caused it to expand from twenty to thirty typescript pages. I made many minor changes, some of which involved thinking through the implications of the chimeras so that the story's internal consistency could be strengthened.

For example, it is stated that eventually the chimeras ossify, become stony. So what about Kumash's final work, which is hanging in the air? In the revised version I specifically mentioned that 'unlike the mobile forms, this one was fixed in the place of its birth'. I also added that 'Kumash had never meant to endow it with either solidity or mass, though it would of course acquire both when it began to ossify, sinking slowly to the earth'. The reader should then be able to infer that even mobile forms gradually lose their powers of movement and turn into statues. With luck, this should suggest that I, the writer, have a full picture of the society I am describing in miniature in the story.

I adopted most of the suggestions for improvement given in the last chapter:

1 Caro is named in the opening sentence, and Vendavo is immediately described as 'Kumash's mentor' when his name is first mentioned to eliminate any confusion between them. It is also made clearer earlier on that Kumash himself is dead.

2 Several references are made to the fact that Caro is deliberately holding her emotions in. She is determined to cope for the sake of the children. For example, she hurries home immediately after the verdict is given, making a deliberate effort to avoid Laaphre. 'He was the kindest of men, but kindness was precisely what she could not bear at the moment: it would crack her like an egg.'

3 The inquest was beefed up considerably, with both Inquestors asking more searching questions, especially about Kumash's behaviour in the days leading up to the murder. This allowed me to flesh out both Kumash and Vendavo a little more, and also to have Caro thinking about her relationship with her husband while the inquest is still continuing, rather than after it as previously. Revising the inquest actually proved to be the major part of the

rewriting, involving the most work because I had to try to re-imagine it from scratch. Eshmei's verdict is now that Kumash murdered Vendavo to immortalise his work through infamy, and the penalty for the crime is the confiscation of his house and all future revenues from his works. Caro at this stage has no idea why her husband killed Vendavo.

4   Two guards are now on duty outside Caro's house prior to the inquest to protect her and her property. They both accompany her to the town, whereupon the mob seize their chance to vandalise the garden. Caro returns home alone to find it in ruins as before.

5   I decided to stick with the idea of Iriyana being Vendavo and Kumash's agent, but I made it clear that her role is 'arranging exhibitions of their work and collecting revenues from the capital' so that there is no ambiguity. Without such a reference, it seems as if the artists' only means of support is through begging bowls, which wasn't entirely plausible. As before, it is Iriyana who points out to Caro that Kumash's final work *is* complete (though it is not suggested that Iriyana understands why Kumash killed Vendavo).

6   Iriyana then returns to town to let Laaphre know that the garden has been vandalised. He dispatches the guards again to protect Caro, and Yanoyal goes with them on this pretext, confronting Caro with his belief that Kumash killed Vendavo to immortalise himself, not his art. Caro slaps him across the face, but then says, 'Yes, that was why he did it' — satisfying him with a lie as before.

7   Caro's understanding of why Kumash killed Vendavo is now more directly tied in with his final chimera. As before, she grasps its meaning, that Kumash was trying to force the half-formed creature back into oblivion. But now she muses: 'Certainly Eshmei was right in that he had been driven by despair, and it was ironic that he probably would achieve a form of immortality through being remembered as Vendavo's murderer. But he hadn't intended that, she was sure. Ultimately he had experienced . . . the betrayal of his talent, the very thing which had powered him through most of his life. His chimeras had failed him through their imperfections, and so he had turned against them and against art in general. In his final despair, it must have seemed to him that Vendavo was responsible for leading him down the path to the ultimate realisation of his inadequacy. And that was why he had murdered him.'

The new ending might seem to be an equally subtle distinction, scarcely worth the attention I have paid to it. But I wouldn't agree. Theme and image are more strongly united and therefore the reader should be left happier that the key to the mystery was given right at the start of the story, when the unfinished work was first described.

Having developed the idea of the chimeras, it seemed to me that I had barely begun to explore their possibilities in this one story. Soon other images and plot-lines were suggesting themselves. For example, could a master-artist like Vendavo create a chimera so life-like that it could not be distinguished from a real human being? Would there be prohibitions in the society against such creations? Could chimeras be made to talk, to play parts in a staged drama of Shakespearian proportions? Why can only some people 'manifest' them? What sort of theories might have been developed to account for the nature of the chimeras? And so on.

There was obviously plenty of scope for development, and eventually I had notions for several stories, all of which would feature Vendavo at different times of his life and would be designed to explore as many facets of the chimeras as possible. Thus, from a single initial idea, a whole fictional world potentially opens up.

Following editorial suggestions which involved trimming the text by the equivalent of a page, the revised story was accepted for publication in the Spring 1988 issue of the British magazine *Interzone*. I continued having problems in finding a suitable title, and finally settled, still not wholly enthusiastically, for 'Artefacts'. I remain convinced that a better title exists somewhere, but so far it has eluded me.

On method

Exactly how a writer revises will depend to a large extent on how the story was originally written. Some writers prefer to get a first draft down as quickly as possible, no matter how rough and ready it is. They then undertake major revisions to get it into shape. Others prefer to proceed slowly, getting every page as right as possible as they go along so that the revisions needed later are minimal. Both approaches may, of course, be used in different stories, or even in different parts of the same story. Writers must discover for themselves which methods suit them best.

It is important to establish some kind of routine for writing regularly. Work for a set number of hours a day? Produce a set number of pages in a given session? The method you choose will depend on your temperament, but give yourself a target *and try to produce regularly*. Writing is often a lonely, frustrating business, and it is very easy to think of excuses not to do it. The important thing is to *finish* the first draft of a story and then go on to *finish* revising it. In other words, follow the creative process through to completion. This can't be overstressed.

Writers' groups

Writers' groups (sometimes called writers' circles or writers' work-shops) can be very useful in suggesting how a story might be revised – provided that you can bear having a story you have lovingly composed dissected by several other individuals. They don't suit everyone, but they do have the bonus that you get a chance to criticise other people's stories as well and so hone your own analytical skills.

How do you become involved in such a group? The simplest way is to organise one yourself with other writers who are at a similar level of experience. Stories (it is better if they are relatively short to begin with) can be sent through the post to other members who will read them and write back comments before forwarding them to the next member. Or you can actually set aside a day in which you will all meet and comment face-to-face on your various contributions.

If you do this, then there are two basic options. The stories can actually be read out at the meeting, to be commented on immediately afterwards. The trouble with this is that it is time-consuming and harder to give a considered opinion of a story that has just been read out to you. A better idea is to circulate your contributions to all other members, preferably a week before the meeting. This allows you time to read all the stories at your leisure and make notes so that on the day of the meeting you are prepared to talk in detail about them.

Here is how a typical meeting might be run.

You decide on a running order – by drawing lots, if necessary. Every person then gives a three-minute critique of a story while its author sits and squirms and takes notes. Afterwards the author has five minutes to respond to the criticisms, in the same frank yet reasonable spirit in which they were given. Then there is a further more informal round of one-minute comments from everyone else to tie things up.

In this way, there is a good chance that a story will be thoroughly analysed in what ideally will be a constructive rather than negative fashion. The three- and five-minute rules may seem rather arbitrary, but they are useful in focusing the mind and making comments crisper. Some sort of time-limit is also necessary for practical reasons. A one-day writers' meeting needs perhaps a minimum of four people but probably no more than eight. Assume six people are attending the meeting.

5 people comment for 3 minutes each on a story	=	15 minutes
the author responds for 5 minutes	=	5 minutes
a further 1-minute response from everyone else	=	5 minutes
a 10-minute break before the next story is criticised	=	10 minutes

That is a total of 35 minutes per story, and thus the whole meeting will last over three hours at minimum. In practice, sessions usually take longer, even when the appointed timekeeper diligently enforces the rules and tells people to wind up their comments if they are over-running. (Often the discussion continues after the formal session has ended, for example.) With seven people the time taken over each story is 39 minutes including the ten-minute break, and the whole session extends to over four hours. With eight people, it is over six hours. And by now, a longer break for food will also be necessary.

Described in this rather bald way, writers' meetings may seem thoroughly daunting and mechanistic. But if criticism is given in a generous and non-partisan spirit it can be immensely valuable. Apart from helping to pinpoint flaws and suggesting means of improvement, it can also teach the writer how to accept criticism without being crushed or becoming hostile. This is something that the writer will almost certainly need in facing up to the even more difficult task of getting work published.

The sf community

That is all very well, you might say, but what if you have no contact with any other writers? If you have the inclination, then contact can be established. Science fiction is a very social genre and many of its readers are active in organising regular conventions attended by writers, editors, agents, and so on. Such conventions are usually held in hotels, over long weekends or whole weeks. Apart from a healthy amount of socialising in the bar, there are usually panel discussions, talks, quizzes, etc. − all of which provide ample opportunities to meet other writers. Science fiction is special in that it has a body of very active readers who have succeeded to an unparalleled extent in breaking down the barriers between themselves and the writers they read. Anyone who buys an sf magazine regularly can usually find details of forthcoming conventions and the addresses of bodies like the Science Fiction Writers of America and the British Science Fiction Association, which in their various ways are committed to promoting science fiction. There is ample scope for making contact with others in the field if you wish.

7
Finding a Publisher

Your story or novel has now been revised to your satisfaction. What next? Assuming that you are hoping to see it published, then the next stage is to prepare a typescript suitable for submission to a magazine or book editor. Unfortunately a manuscript lovingly handwritten in quill pen or green ball-point is not acceptable these days, so a typewriter (or word-processor) must be used at this final stage.

If you can't type, then you may be able to find someone else to do it for you. But it is best to learn yourself if you are serious about writing as a career. It is not necessary to be able to touch-type (I myself use only two fingers and both thumbs) though this does help speed and accuracy. Speed isn't usually important in fiction, but reasonable neatness and accuracy are.

Preparation of typescript

Stories should be typed on one side of unlined white paper (typically A4 size in Britain and American quarto in the USA), double-spaced and with good margins on both sides of the page. Aim for between 20 and 30 lines per page as a rough guide, with ten to fifteen words on a full line, depending on the size of your typeface. The title page of your story should carry your name and address (ditto the last page if you wish). Each page should be numbered, and each can also carry the title of the story (or an abbreviated version of it) though this isn't vital.

Neatness does not imply spotlessness. Typing errors are best corrected by xxx-ing out the error and retyping the revision above rather than daubing on pools of liquid paper. (Double-spacing allows sufficient room for such revisions to be made.) Handwritten corrections should be kept to a minimum. The important thing is that the typescript does not look messy and that it is legible. (Oddly enough, it is an old saw in publishing circles that an immaculate typescript, often splendidly bound, usually proves to be very badly written.) Editors face great demands on their time and attention, and they won't dwell long on an unsolicited typescript if it is badly typed or scrawled with handwritten corrections or has been typed with a faded ribbon so that the words can scarcely be made out.

Always keep a copy of any story you write, plus a copy of any covering letter, dated so that you know when the story was sent out. A carbon copy is the least expensive, though if you have access to cheap photocopying facilities, or use a word-processor which can turn out multiple copies, then this may be more convenient.

The covering letter

A covering letter should be brief and factual, saying that you enclose such-and-such for consideration. *Don't* extol the brilliance of what you have written or try to win the editor over with flattery, bribes, threats or jokes. Editors are professionals who are paid to use their own judgement, and they are more likely to be put off than won over by such tactics. As far as possible, let the story speak for itself.

If your story is not accepted for publication and you would like it returned to you, then enclose a self-addressed envelope with return postage – and mention that you have done so in the covering letter. Apart from anything else, this is only polite. Publishers will sometimes return rejected stories even if covering postage hasn't been sent, but many won't; the material will be thrown away instead.

On literary agents

So far we have assumed that you are intending to submit your story direct to an editor. But if you have written a novel, you might consider first approaching a literary agent. (Most agents don't handle short stories – even whole collections – unless the writer is already established or shows exceptional talent in that form.)

Literary agents, as their name suggests, are the author's representatives, and the first thing to say about them is that they take a cut (usually ten per cent, called *commission*) of the proceeds of any sale to a publisher. Finding a good agent is often just as hard as finding a good publisher; you have to satisfy the agent, just as you have to satisfy an editor, that your work is good enough for them to want to represent you. It also helps if you like one another personally, for although a writer's partnership with an agent is a business one, it should ideally be somewhat more than that, the agent offering advice and support and generally helping to protect the writer against some of the harsher realities of publishing.

The advantages of having an agent are several:

1   Any novel submitted to a publisher by an agent is likely to be given more serious (and swifter) consideration by an editor than if it came from the author alone. The editor immediately knows that it has been read and liked by at least one other person.

2   Agents have a wide-ranging knowledge of the publishing market and personal contact with editors so that they are able to send the novel to suitable publishers and able also to badger editors who are being dilatory.

3   They can often get more money out of a publisher by striking a harder bargain than the author could alone (and so cover their commission and more).

4   They are (or should be) expert at negotiating contracts which ensure that the author's legal rights are protected and potential earnings maximised.

5   They have contacts overseas with agents and publishers, and so foreign rights in a book are often more easily sold.

Most professional authors have agents, though very often it is easier to find one *after* you have had work published. *Literary Market Place* lists many of them, and the sf writer needs one who has some enthusiasm for science fiction and some knowledge of the special requirements of the sf market.

Choosing your market

Let us assume you haven't got an agent and are going to submit your work yourself. A short story will probably be sent to the editor of an sf magazine, a novel to a fiction editor at a publishing house. Similar rules apply: neat typescript, brief covering letter, return postage enclosed if you want the typescript back. (Novels can be bound or put loose-leafed into a folder or an old typing-paper box. Many editors prefer loose-leafed submissions. Fat, tightly bound typescripts often have to be taken apart before they can be read, and editors are never impressed by fancy binding alone.)

Before you submit anything, *study the market*. It would be a waste of time sending 'hard' technologically based science fiction to an outlet that specialises in fantasy, for example. Read several issues of any magazine before you submit a short story to it; read several novels on a publisher's list before you send in your own. And make sure they are recent issues or novels. Editors come and go, and publishing policies may alter as a consequence. A magazine may suddenly change the content and emphasis of its fiction in response to declining sales; a particular publisher with a strong sf list might suddenly stop publishing it altogether if an incoming fiction editor has no affinity with the genre.

All of this is not to suggest that you should studiously tailor your work to the market. Write it first without thinking of any specific outlet; then, when it is finished, look to see where it might find the best home or at least the most sympathetic reading. There are few things more frustrating than having a story turned down because it doesn't fit publishing policies: this still leaves unanswered the question of whether the story is any good in its own right.

Portrait of the editor as a harassed man

Suppose you have recently completed your first novel, over which you have laboured long and hard for a year or two or more. Finally you have revised it to your satisfaction, typed it up neatly and are ready to send it off to the publisher of your choice. You think it is going to knock the editor's socks off and make all other publishers envious that you didn't send it to them first. You will be fêted, acclaimed as a brilliant new discovery, have a glorious career ahead of you. So you parcel it up with a polite covering letter and send it off. A week passes, and then you start to anticipate a rapturous phonecall from the editor (you thoughtfully gave your telephone number in the covering letter). A further week goes by. Perhaps he (or she) will write you an ecstatic letter instead. Another week passes. Then another. Then another. Gloom begins to descend.

The chances are that he hasn't even looked at your novel yet, and won't do so for another several weeks – at least. He may be a science fiction expert, but it is just as likely to be only one of the many types of book which he has to consider – romances, historical novels, detective novels, mysteries, thrillers, and so on.

Here he is, sitting in his little office, desk piled high with books and typescripts, shelves piled high with books and typescripts, floor entirely covered with books and typescripts. Meanwhile agents, irate authors, the publicity department, cover artists, accounts people, his mother are constantly ringing up to complain that he is neglecting them. A best-selling author is annoyed because her name was too small on the cover of her latest book; a noveliser of a TV series hasn't been paid his publication money; an ambitious agent is suddenly demanding twice the agreed advance for her client's latest blockbuster; the editorial director needs a writer found to do a book in three weeks on the sex-life of hamsters; one of the secretaries has just walked in with another armful of unsolicited typescripts. . . .

An extreme example? Not especially. Paperback houses, in particular, tend to be swamped by submissions – hardback novels for paperback sale, foreign novels, commissioned novels awaiting reading and editing, submissions from agents, and finally the slush pile – the unflattering name given to typescripts sent in by unknown authors. As likely as not, the neatly typed science fiction novel is sitting at the bottom of one of the piles on the floor.

So what happens next? Usually (sooner rather than later if the editor is efficient) it will be pulled out of the pile and given a quick scan. Assuming that it is not obviously incompetent, then it will probably be sent to a publisher's reader – a freelance individual who will read it and write a short report summarising its plot and its flaws or virtues. If either the author's covering letter or the editor's quick scan has identified it as a science fiction novel, then it will be sent to a reader specialising in sf. He or she will make a recommendation as to whether the novel should be considered for publication.

If the reader's report is unfavourable, then the novel will probably be sent back to the author with a polite letter of rejection. If favourable, the battle is not yet won. The editor may then take a look at it, reading as much as he needs to convince himself that it isn't suitable for publication. If this sounds very negative, it is merely another way of saying that a first novel from an unknown author has everything to prove.

Sometimes an editor will see flaws that can be corrected and so will read on to the end; sometimes he will read on to the end but still decide that the novel isn't publishable. Or – happy day – he may be satisfied that it would be a valuable addition to the publisher's list. In which case he will probably mention it at the next editorial meeting and do his damnedest to persuade his colleagues that an offer should be made to the author. Should others agree that the novel is worth publishing, then its sales potential will be assessed before it is decided what advance will be offered for the right to publish the book. At last the longed-for letter will be sent to the author, usually some months or more after the novel was first sent in.

With short story submissions to magazines, the process is usually simpler, the editor often reading everything and giving a yes or no within weeks. Again, though, magazine editors sometimes have paid readers to vet unsolicited stories from unknown writers. Turn-around is generally faster because magazines publish more frequently and need to clear their backlog regularly. And of course reading a six-thousand word story takes less time than a sixty-thousand word novel.

How to get your work read faster

There is really no sure-fire means of doing this. Some editors are determinedly slow, and nothing can stir them out of their sloth-like torpor. But a useful tip is to address your submission to a *named* editor rather than simply a given publisher (or magazine) alone. If you don't know the editor's name, then a phonecall to the publisher will usually provide it (ask for the name of the editor who deals with science fiction). A typescript sent to a specific person will often be read more quickly because it suggests to the editor that you have taken the trouble to investigate the market thoroughly.

If you hear nothing from a publisher after three months, then write a polite letter explaining that you submitted a novel on a particular date and would welcome a decision. If you have still heard nothing after six months, then write firmly but still politely asking if your typescript could be returned to you. Few publishers return submissions completely unread, and the chances are that your novel will receive hasty if belated consideration.

Letters of rejection

These are a depressingly familiar occurrence to most writers, especially to begin with. They are also frustrating because they seldom say anything useful about *why* the story or novel was rejected. Editors tend to favour bland phrases such as 'does not meet our requirements', 'read it with interest but feel unable to make an offer', and so on. In other words, there is no analysis of where the story or novel was felt to fail.

This is not entirely surprising. Editors don't have the time for detailed critical comments which might in any case prompt the author to disagree indignantly, creating much ill-will to no fruitful purpose. Expect no more than a brief regretful paragraph, though if the rejection letter happens to add that the publisher would be interested in seeing any of your future work, then you can justifiably feel that you have made some impression and should try again when you have something new to offer.

Hardback or paperback?

Most short stories are submitted to magazines or, occasionally, to original anthologies produced by a publisher and edited by one or more people who actually select the stories. With novels, the writer has the choice of first approaching either a hardback or a paperback publisher.

Each has different advantages and disadvantages. A hardback edition of a novel is obviously more durable than a paperback, and there is also more chance of the book being reviewed in newspapers and magazines, whose reviewers often treat original paperbacks sketchily, if at all. The hardback publisher who agrees to accept a novel may then arrange a paperback edition with another publisher, and this edition will appear some time after the hardback. A portion of the proceeds of the paperback edition will usually be taken by the hardback publisher in such cases.

Original paperback editions have the advantage that the advance paid for the book is often larger than for a hardback edition. Hardbacks sell mainly to libraries, whereas paperbacks are bought by the reading public, and so you reach a paying audience more quickly (though the Public Lending Right bill in Britain ensures that authors now earn some income from books borrowed from libraries). On the other hand, paperbacks are more ephemeral, and may be displayed on a bookseller's shelves for only a month or two, if that. The paperback market is more volatile, and in general it is easier to establish a long-term professional relationship with a hardback house, who will usually want to publish your work consistently once they have made an initial investment in you as a writer.

On contracts

Space doesn't allow a detailed discussion of the labyrinthine complexities of many publishers' contracts, but a few salient points can be noted. If a publisher makes an offer for your story or novel, it essentially means that money will be paid for the right to publish it. In shorthand, the writer 'sells' a story to a magazine or a novel to a publishing house. But, in fact, writers don't actually sell their work at all: they *lease* it to the publisher, and the terms of that lease are what is outlined in the contract. They give the publisher certain *rights* in the use of the story or novel.

Each of these rights belongs to you until you sell it to a publisher. At no time does the story or novel itself cease to be your property, but there is always a danger that the contract (more formally, a 'Memorandum of Agreement') may not specify clearly enough the precise extent of the publisher's usage of your work. One of the main jobs of the literary agent is to ensure that the terms of the contract are clearly defined and the author's rights protected. If you sell 'world rights' in something, for example, this means that the publisher is now free to sell the work anywhere else, without consulting you; if you sell only British or American Rights, then you (or your agent) are free to negotiate separate sales in other countries.

Contracts are complex legal documents which would need a full chapter or more to do them any justice. To the new writer who has just sold a first novel, the most important thing is often the size of the *advance*. This is what the publisher agrees to pay you to begin with – it is an advance against *royalties*, which are in turn the author's percentage of the revenue from the sales of a book.

Say a paperback publisher pays you an advance of £2000 ($3500). Standard royalty rates vary, but for the sake of simplicity let us assume you are offered a figure of 10% of the selling price of the book.* When the novel is finally published it retails at £2 ($3.50) a copy. The author on a 10% royalty is therefore entitled to 20p (35c) on every book sold. But the publisher has already paid an advance of £2000 ($3500), and therefore the book will need to sell over 10,000 copies before it earns its advance and the writer starts to receive royalties.

Royalties are usually calculated on an incremental scale, the percentage increasing with increased sales. With first novels, the publisher will hope but not necessarily expect that the book will earn out its advance. Often the publisher will be sure of making a loss (preferably a small one) on the deal but will see it as worthwhile because it is an investment in an author who may gradually build up a reputation or suddenly make a breakthrough that will pay handsome dividends.

Advances to authors are seldom paid in one lump sum. More commonly they are paid in two or three parts, typically half on signature of the contract and half on publication of the book.

How long does it take for a book to be published?

The usual time-scale is six to eighteen months, though occasionally it is shorter and sometimes lamentably longer. If we assume an average of one year, then a standard advance for a book (say £2000 in Britain) won't provide anywhere near a living wage. Of course, overseas sales of the same book may boost that figure considerably, but these can't necessarily be relied on. The author will need to be either very prolific or very frugal in order to survive on the income from writing alone.

*In practice, royalty rates are usually between 5% and 7½% to begin with.

Financial rewards probably won't matter immediately. There is nothing quite like the pleasure of finally receiving copies of your first book (or seeing your first story in a magazine). You may hate the cover illustration, feel that the publisher's synopsis of the book on the back or inside flap of the dust-jacket is totally awful (these will probably be matters over which you will have little, if any, influence), but you finally have something concrete to show for all your endeavours.

What are sf editors and publishers looking for?

The short answer to this is that they don't really know until they see it in front of them. (This applies to all kinds of fiction, not just sf.) Which isn't meant to suggest that editors and publishers are brainless, merely that they are limited in what they can publish by what is actually submitted to them. Ultimately it is up to the authors to supply the product. Publishing is a business, but it isn't the same as marketing cans of baked beans (though many disgruntled writers would see it as just that). Of course books are often commissioned on specific subjects, and bestsellers can be created by a combination of astute hard-headed writing and skilful editing. But it is always a gamble, with uncertain results. In the end, publishers understand no better than anyone else why one book sells but not another.

In my experience, publishers are generally conservative in their tastes, with occasional bursts of wild adventurism and a modicum of philanthropy. Which is to say that they will usually publish anything by established authors who are guaranteed to sell, will sometimes pay ridiculously large amounts of money for books which cannot possibly hope to cover their advances, and will periodically publish books which they know to be uncommercial but which they feel deserve an audience, no matter how small.

The encouraging thing for the new writer is that there is always room on a publisher's list. Even bestselling authors go out of fashion or come to the end of their creative life. In addition, the real world is always changing, and publishers need authors who have their fingers on the pulse of contemporary life. New writers are the life-blood of any publisher's list in the long term; without them, the list eventually dies.

This is as true in science fiction as anywhere else, and it should encourage the new writer to struggle on against all the obstacles which usually lie ahead. Work hard, be prepared to learn from your mistakes, and try to maintain confidence in your abilities. And, above all, *persevere.* The material rewards are seldom great, but writing offers many other forms of satisfaction which are unique.

Afterword

Writing a book of this nature is an act of hubris: it is far easier to preach the principles of good writing than to practise them yourself. To me, this book was largely an exercise in confronting many of my own limitations as a writer of science fiction and of suggesting to myself ways in which I might overcome them. Hope springs eternal in the author's breast. . . .

A number of people helped either directly or indirectly with the writing of this book, and I would like to thank: Brian Aldiss, Faith Brooker, Randal Flynn, David Garnett, Robert Holdstock, Garry Kilworth, Bobbie Lamming, Lisa Tuttle and David Wingrove, plus all the authors actually quoted in the book. Needless to say, none of them is responsible for the opinions I have expressed.

Index